INDIAN ALCHEMY
OR
RASAYANA

IN THE LIGHT OF ASCETICISM AND GERIATRICS

INDIAN ALCHEMY
OR
RASAYANA

IN THE LIGHT OF ASCETICISM AND GERIATRICS

S. MAHDIHASSAN

MOTILAL BANARSIDASS PUBLISHERS
PVT. LTD. • DELHI

First Edition: Delhi, 1977
Second Revised Edition: Delhi, 1991

ISBN: 81-208-0788-x

Also available at:
MOTILAL BANARSIDASS
41 U.A., Bungalow Road, Jawahar Nagar, Delhi 110 007
120 Royapettah High Road, Mylapore, Madras 600 004
16 St. Mark's Road, Bangalore 560 001
Ashok Rajpath, Patna 800 004
Chowk, Varanasi 221 001

PRINTED IN INDIA
BY JAINENDRA PRAKASH JAIN AT SHRI JAINENDRA PRESS, A-45 NARAINA INDUSTRIAL AREA, PHASE I, NEW DELHI 110 028 AND PUBLISHED BY NARENDRA PRAKASH JAIN FOR MOTILAL BANARSIDASS PUBLISHERS PVT. LTD., BUNGALOW ROAD, JAWAHAR NAGAR, DELHI 110 007

DEDICATED

To

SIR JOSEPH NEEDHAM, SC.D., F.R.S., F.B.A.
Director, Needham Research Institute, Cambridge,
author of the classical work "Science and Civilization in China",
in seven volumes, as token of gratitude for appreciating my
humble work in a way which no one has done so far.

CONTENTS

I. FOREWORD BY H.E. PROF. S.H. NASR CHANCELLOR: ARYAMEHR UNIVERSITY, TEHRAN — XI

II. INTRODUCTION — XVI

PARAGRAPHS — *PAGES*

1. DIFFERENTIAL APPROACH OF A SCIENTIST AND A HISTORIAN — 1
2. THE AGENCIES ON WHICH ALCHEMY DEPENDED — 2
3. OTHER LACUNAE IN THE ACCOUNTS OF ALCHEMY — 2
4. CARDINAL POINTS OF KNOWLEDGE — 4
5. THE POSITIVE CRITERION OF ALCHEMY AS A WHOLE — 4
6. TIMES THAT MADE ALCHEMY — 5
7. SOCIAL LIFE CREATED ASCETICISM AND THIS IN TURN AN URGE FOR REJUVENATION — 6
8. BIRTH OF HERBALISM — 9
9. THE FIRST NEED OF THE ASCETIC FOR AN ENERGIZER — 10
10. COMPARATIVE PHARMACOLOGY OF ENERGIZERS — 12
11. SOMA AS FRESH PLANT JUICE AND ITS HERB — 14
12. THE POSITION OF RASAYANA IN INDIAN MEDICINE — 16
13. PREHISTORIC COSMOGONY SUPPORTING THE IDEA OF REJUVENATION — 19
14. CHARAKA AND HIS TWO CATEGORIES OF MEDICINE — 20
15. HERBAL RASAYANAS — 21
16. METALLIC PREPARATIONS AS RASAYANA — 24
17. CHARAKA EXTOLLING IRON AND A REDUCING AGENT — 25

PARAGRAPHS *PAGES*

18. CHARAKA'S INCIDENTAL MENTION OF A GOLD PREPARATION 26
19. SILAJIT OR MINERAL PITCH VITALIZER 27
20. CALCINED METALS AS PHLOGISTON 29
21. CALCINED METALS AS ALCHEMICAL PREPARATIONS 29
22. THE LEGEND OF PHOENIX AS IMPLYING RESURRECTION 32
23. GROWTH VERSUS REPRODUCTION 33
24. GROWTH INTRINSIC TO MATTER 36
25. ANIMISM VERSUS DUALISM 38
26. THE TWO SUB-SOULS 39
27. PULVERIZATION OF CALCINED METALS 42
28. CALCINED GOLD AS THE IDEAL HERBO-METALLIC PREPARATION 42
29. OTHER SYSTEMS OF GAINING LONGEVITY 45
30. THE BEGINNING OF ALCHEMY 46
31. HERBALISM IN CHINA AS PROGENITOR OF ALCHEMY 48
32. KASHMIR AS CONNECTING INDIA WITH CHINA 49
33. INDIAN ALCHEMY PROBABLY BEGINS ABOUT 500 A.D. 50
34. ALCHEMY IN INDIA ABOUT 1000 A.D. 51
35. MOMIYAI A PANACEA OF LATER ORIGIN IN INDIA 53
36. DRUG-INDUCED SUBLIMATION OF THE MATERIAL BODY 56
37. LEGENDS OF GOLD WITH THE POWER OF GROWTH 57
38. ETYMOLOGY OF RASAYANA 60
39. RASAYANA AS ELIXIR 63
40. KIMIYA-ELIXIR 65
41. DRUGS OF REJUVENATION, CHINESE AND INDIAN, AS REACHING ALEXANDRIA 66
42. RASAYANA AS A PROPER NAME 73

PARAGRAPHS *PAGES*

43. RASAYANA AS SHIVA, THE RESURRECTOR, IN THE HINDU TRINITY 76

44. MERCURIALS AS DRUGS OF CHOICE IN ACQUIRING REJUVENATION 81

45. MAKARADHWAJA OR CUPID'S HALLMARK 88

46. MERCURY AS RELATED TO SHIVA IN INDIAN MYTHOLOGY 89

47. PERSISTENCE OF HERBALISM IN MERCURIAL ALCHEMY 90

48. SHIVA AS HERMAPHRODITE AND CREATOR 91

49. SHIVA AS RELATED TO BRAHMA AND VISHNU 95

50. DRUGS OF LONGEVITY VERSUS OF IMMORTALITY 98

51. THE NATURE OF ACTIVE PRINCIPLE IN DRUGS OF IMMORTALITY 100

52. SUBLIMATING SUB-SOULS AS PRELUDE TO UNION OF OPPOSITES 100

53. THE ONE ORIGIN OF CREATIVE POWER 102

54. LEGENDS IMPLYING ALCHEMY AS INITIATING CREATION 103

55. DUALISM VERSUS PANTHEISM AND ALCHEMY 104

56. POSITIVE CONCEPTION OF SUB-SOULS 106

57. SYMBOLISM REVEALING ALCHEMY AS IMITATING CREATION 109

58. CONCORDANCE BETWEEN INDIAN MEDICINE AND INDIAN PHILOSOPHY 113

59. UNION OF OPPOSITES AS A PRACTICAL DOCTRINE 116

60. JABIR'S MAGIC SQUARE AND THE IMPORTANCE OF ITS FOUR NUMBERS 117

SUMMARY 121

BIBLIOGRAPHY 125

EXPLANATION OF FIGURES 135

FIGURES 138

Note : The numbers within brackets given in the text denote references as given in the bibliography. The first number indicates the serial number in bibliography and subsequent numbers the volume and page numbers.

FOREWORD

BY

DR. SEYYED HOSSEIN NASR

The study of alchemy during the past century in the West has been dominated for the most part by a scientistic spirit that is totally impervious to the extra-spatial dimensions of reality and blind to the language of symbolism through which the higher states of being reveal themselves within the matrix of the spatio-temporal world. Except for a few out-standing works such as the penetrating study of Titus Burckhardt,[1] most modern writings have tried to reduce alchemy to a proto-chemistry or at best a psychology which is, however, divorced from the world of the Spirit. Alchemy is of course related to a science of the soul and is also inextricably bound in certain of its aspects to the early history of chemistry and metallurgy. But it cannot be reduced to either the study of materials pure and simple or of the psyche divorced from pneuma. It is a science that is directly related to the extra-spatial and temporal levels of the universal hierarchy and therefore totally beyond the reach of any of the profane methods employed during the past century in its study.

Strangely enough, there has been a great deal of interest in alchemy of late as a result of the appearance

---

[1]. Published originally in German as *Alchemie; Sinn und Welt-bild*, Olten, 1960; and translated later into English by W. Stoddard as *Alchemy : Science of the Cosmos, Science of the Soul*, London, 1967 and Baltimore, 1972, and into French as *Alchimie : Sa signification et son image du monde*. Basel, 1974.

of fissures in the walls of the closed world created by classical 17th century science and its aftermath. Works on alchemy are now read by a much wider audience than a generation ago and are no longer confined to either historians of science or occultists. And for this very reason the need for serious treatment of the subject is felt ever more widely. The search for a true understanding of alchemy today is related to the general quest on the part of many well-intentioned people for a re-discovery of tradition and the recovery of a new harmonious relationship with nature, although many do not realize that the understanding of such cosmological sciences as alchemy is impossible without the light of the metaphysical doctrines of which all cosmological sciences are applications.[2]

Alchemy is one of the principal traditional cosmological sciences, cultivated in one form or another in all traditional societies—at least those of a sedentary nature—for thousands of years before the dawn of recorded history and systematized into a formulated science in Alexandria, China and India at least two thousand years ago. It is a science of the cosmos and of the soul, related at once to cosmology, the process of spiritual realization and hence traditional psychology,[3] medicine, metallurgy, chemistry and also art. It is based on the perspective that there is something of everything in everything and that through the presence of the sacred a transformation can take place within things which changes their very substance and not only

---

2. We have dealt fully with this question in our *An Introduction to Islamic Cosmological Doctrines*, Cambridge (U.S.A.), 1964, second edition, London, 1970; and *Science and Civilization in Islam*, Cambridge, (U.S.A.), 1968 and New York, 1970.

3. Following A.K. Coomaraswamy we would call it pneumatology rather than psychology. See Coomaraswamy, "On the Indian and Traditional Psychology, or rather Pneumatology", in *Selected Writings of Ananda K. Coomaraswamy*, ed. by R. Lipsey, Princeton.

their accidents. The alchemical perspective has been directly concerned on the one hand with minerals, metals and aurification, with all that the element gold symbolizes in the natural domain. On the other hand it has also been closely associated with the question "immortality" and "longevity" and ultimately with the acquiring of the "body of gold" or "diamond", which is also the goal of initiatic techniques. In some civilizations the one aspect has been emphasized, and in others the other. But seen from the highest point of view and in the light of the most universal principles of alchemy it can be said that there is a profound unity within the alchemical perspective, whether one is dealing with Alexandrian, Chinese, Indian, Islamic or Western alchemy.

As far as Indian alchemy, the subject of the present book, is concerned, it is one of the main branches of the "tree of alchemy" and yet has received less attention, in the West at least, than Alexandrian or even Chinese alchemy. The earlier historians of alchemy such as von Lippmann believed that alchemy was brought to India by Muslims. Later research has unveiled references to alchemy ante-dating the rise of Islam, and it is now conceded by most scholars that Indian alchemy has a much more ancient history than imagined until now and that it is in fact closely related to certain forms of Yoga, especially Tantrism, with which it became closely associated later, to the extent that the power to perform alchemical transmutation came to be considered as one of the *siddhis* of Yogis. The influence of Islamic alchemy in the Indian world was a later factor which complemented an already existing tradition.

Considering the dearth of material on Indian alchemy, it is with pleasure that one welcomes the appearance of the present work by Dr. Mahdihassan whose research on Chinese and Islamic alchemy is already known to students of the field. Dr. Mahdihassan is to be especially congratulated for making clear the nexus between alchemy and medicine, a relation that is often disregarded by those accustomed to the well-known studies of Alexandrian alchemy with their sole emphasis upon the mineralogical and the metallurgical aspects of alchemy. Dr. Mahdihassan has already written many informative articles and essays on the origins of the word "alchemy" the use of the word *Kimiya'* in Arabic and Persian as the name of a substance rather than only the name of the royal art, the relation between Chinese and Islamic alchemy and many other related subjects, stressing over and over again the rapport between alchemy and medicine. He has thus helped to re-establish the balance that should exist in seeing alchemy as being related to the mineral world on the one hand and the world of plants on the other, both of course acting as foundations for concerns that ultimately belong to another domain of reality.[4]

It is this perspective which Dr. Mahdihassan applied to his study of *Rasayana* or Indian alchemy, which he sees essentially as geriatrics and closely bound to the life of ascetics in the wilderness and elderly people left by themselves in remote places. There has been without doubt a relationship from the very beginning between initiatic and spiritual practices on the one hand and the external "substances" used to attain health, longevity and immortality on the other, a relationship which becomes fully manifest in later Indian history. Dr. Mahdihassan is not concerned so much with this relation as with the medico-pharmaceutical practices which have always accompanied alchemy in India as well as in Tibet and China, not to speak of certain schools of Islamic alchemy. To this concern he

[4]. To this day there are practising alchemists in Persia in such cities as Isfahan who consider alchemy to be concerned with both medicine and mineralogy and metallurgy and who are known for their prowess in treating diseases as in practising aurification.

brings a great deal of learning and experience providing much material that is fresh and is made available for the first time in an easily attainable source.

The present work is, therefore, a valuable addition to the literature of alchemy and provides another perspective from which Indian alchemy and through it Chinese and even Islamic alchemy can be studied. It is our hope that this and similar works will provide the constitutive elements from which a complete and total picture of the science of alchemy can be constructed, a science that is concerned at once with the cosmos and the soul, with minerals and plants, and finally with the healing art and the art of making things. Dr. Mahdi-hassan is to be congratulated for providing valuable material for the creation of the total image of that arcane discipline which is at once an art and a science and which deals ultimately with man himself as a substance that is to be transmuted and made worthy of the immortality for which he is destined through his own theomorphic nature.

INTRODUCTION

In a preface the author is privileged to relate that part of his autobiography which pertains to the book. The subject made a strong appeal to me in so far as a chemist should know the early history of his science which is alchemy. I have therefore not spared any energy collecting authentic views, contacting contemporary alchemists, who were only a few, as surviving authorities, and critically deducing conclusions, finally all presented in this monograph. On the whole I feel it is as good an account as I can offer at the moment. But the tragedy of what is good is that there can be something better. I myself could have improved upon what is offered here if I had access to the selected literature I had accumulated during several years. Among them were reprints of valuable articles, correspondence and publications of three authorities to whom I am indebted for much information as also for encouragement. They are Prof. J. Needham of Cambridge, Prof. W. Pagel of London and Prof. Kashikar of Poona. All this literature was at Pabna, Bangladesh, but my residence was looted. I had therefore to start my work afresh and I am aware it is neither the last word on the subject nor the last but one. Prof. Graubard has kindly presented me a copy of his valuable book, "Astrology and Alchemy, as two fossil sciences." Biologists however feel justified, in some cases, to use the paradoxical term, "living fossil". I am presenting alchemy here as a "living fossil" of culture and I feel this alone suffices to justify my thesis.

The one point where I radically differ with most authorities is the basic idea on which alchemy is founded. The entire play of alchemy depends upon the idea of soul. In this connection I have tried to follow Animism, Dualism and Monism as would be interpreted by their orthodox adherents. Others have tried to rationalize what by nature is incapable of such an approach. For instance soul is a sort of code-word for what essentially differentiates the living and the dead. The Chinese use the word Ch'i for it. In the pages that follow soul is looked upon as the power which is all-becoming, all-changing and, above all, enabling things to grow and reproduce. For the purpose of history of alchemy this definition fully suffices. Creation proceeded from a primordial soul and the Universe was its incarnation. The alchemists, Islamic and European, conceived it as primordial substance, Prime Matter. The Cosmic Soul and Prime Matter are two phases of the same entity. One is reminded here of Oswald who pronounced that, matter is what we know and energy is what we think. Today we admit matter can change into energy and vice versa. Accordingly Ch'i or Soul is what the ancients believed the entity to be, and Prime Matter what the alchemists tried to know as the source of existence. Our popular notion of creation starts with two entities, the word of God contacting a clod of earth, which begins to grow and shape itself as though the clod had become an embryo. The alchemist tried to rehearse creation with two corresponding opposites. Soul was extracted from donors richly endowed with it, as plants are, and infused it in solid vehicles like metals. Thereby they started with two opposites, a delicate herb but rich in soul, and a metal, inert but heat-resistant, as its future vehicle. The resultant represented soul transferred into a metal. Just as soul made a clod of earth grow into Adam, herbal soul incorporated into a metal made this a ferment, which means it could grow and increase. A calcined metal was a herbo-metallic complex but, as is being explained here, also a hermaphrodite by constitution, and autonomous by function as a ferment. The best preparation deserved to be called Ferment-gold. It was perfect in so far as gold, the vehicle, is fire-proof. And it is fire-proof because it grows so fast that any injury due to heat is repaired at the same time. Ferment-gold, however, cannot resist the high temperature at which gold melts. Ferment-gold was live-gold, heat-resistant, but not fire-proof whereas gold as metal is fire-proof. Let us here consider awards of honour e. g. bronze-medal and gold-medal. It is the "medal" that is of real importance and not the metal. Yet the judge feels justified in selecting for the best award a vehicle which is the most permanent of all metals. Likewise when the alchemist has changed a base metal, say once into silver, and on another occasion into gold, he has produced in the latter case a superior drug. He could claim his art having reached the stage of perfection for gold as a metal is fire-proof whereas silver is not. Extending this idea when silver is enlivened, as Ferment-silver, and gold, as Ferment-gold, the latter must obviously be better in every respect. To talk of live-metals or calcined metals as resurrected metals, representing "Resurrection Bodies", shocks modern rationalists. Such authors trying to modernize ideas based on Animism and Dualism have given us a distorted picture of alchemy. In as much as the alchemists have suffered thereby I have fears that my own interpretations may meet the same fate. I have therefore felt it expedient to repeat myself though it is detrimental to style. But I have left nothing vague and defined such terms as "perfection" and even "soul". Altogether I feel that the contents presented here will offer a correct picture of alchemy. Above all it will indicate that it is very much alive and a panacea, called Makara Dhwaja, is available in India as a preparation of synthetic cinnabar and cinnabar was taken orally in

China as early as 200 B. C. and was used as a drug of resurrection about 600 B.C., if not even earlier.

It is assumed that the human mind loves to be entertained by legends and mythologies. Legends start popularizing new ideas in a beautiful form. After alchemy was introduced, but not yet popular, as in the days when Alberuni lived in India, legends existed implying gold as a live-metal capable of growth and self-repair. The full impact of alchemy upon mythology remodelled god Shiva so that we can say, alchemy modified Shiva before Shiva modified Rasayana, thereby creating alchemy in India. From Rasayana, as "Indian alchemy", we finally come to real "alchemy in India", the former was herbal in origin, the latter mercurial, both preparing drugs of immortality.

The feature which took most of my energy was to show correspondence between "two opposites" as co-creators, upon which theoretical alchemy is based, and the "two pillars" of Indian philosophy, Brahman and Atman, as the two fractions of soul as a whole. Brahman is identified as Growth-soul or male sub-soul, and Atman as Soul-corporeal or female sub-soul. Their union means fusion of opposites which results in creative energy capable of conferring rejuvenation, resurrection and immortality. For it to change and enliven a metal into Ferment-gold is a trivial achievement. Indian philosophy is made to explain theoretical alchemy since both are founded on Dualism merging into Monism. The conception of a ferment, dual-natured but as one and that of a hermaphrodite, indissoluble and as one, show how Dualism developed into Monism. In Indian Monism, Brahman incarnates itself into Atman; they are like mirror images, they are not identical, just as two poles of a magnet are not, yet one cannot exist without the other. With such attempts I feel I could not have gone deeper into theoretical alchemy bringing Indian Rasayana and Indian Upanishads, each unique in nature, together as the products of the same thinker. Holding such views I certainly do not endorse the popular view of the origin of alchemy pronounced by authors like A. G. Hopkins, who writes that, "in the beginning alchemy was far from being philosophical; it was just an art like that of the carpenter or black-smith". Here it is being shown that the ascetic, hankering after rejuvenation, founded Rasayana which developed into alchemy and, hankering after immortality, established Upanishadic philosophy. Lust for life made the individual dream of eternal youth in this world and took him to Rasayana and alchemy. Another who realized this as impossible and feared death became an idealist and aspired for a place in heaven, among the immortals, and the way leading to it took to Vedanta, as "applied philosophy," philosophy of immortality.

That part of the book which is written last and yet read before the book itself is the Foreword. This is best written by one who knows the subject and also the author. It is an honour and a source of happiness for me that His Excellency the Chancellor of Aryamehr University of Technology, Teheran, Iran, Prof. Dr. Seyyed Hossein Nasr, a renowned scholar, has kindly contributed the Foreword. I beg to dedicate the monograph to Dr. J. Needham, FRS., the world's leading authority on the History of Chinese Science and Technique for kindly appreciating my past work in a way which no one has done so far. It is my pleasant duty to thank both these authorities once again here.

The monograph has resulted as a labour of love. I am fortunate that it is being published by the Institute of History of Medicine and Medical Research, New Delhi, whose President, Hakim Abdul Hameed Sahib has also dedicated himself to advance such knowledge for its own sake. Naturally he has placed me under a great debt of gratitude. I must also thank Mr. Jawed Mirza for his patience and perseverance in typing the manuscript.

S. MAHDIHASSAN

INDIAN ALCHEMY OR RASAYANA IN THE LIGHT OF ASCETICISM AND GERIATRICS

1. Differential approach of a scientist and a historian.

Alchemy has been a science of some sort and it also claims a history. Accordingly, if we approach its past, we are called upon to do justice to it, first as a scientist and next as a historian. The historian seems to be mainly concerned with events and his anxiety is limited to their documentation. What leads to events does not seem to interest him. Let us consider two decisive battles of the world. One at Waterloo as a crushing defeat of the French which could properly account for the subsequent changes in the face of Europe. The other was fought, in 1757, at Plassey, in India, which relatively was a skirmish. And Clive, who was victorious, reported to his authorities in England that, "fortunately there was little loss of life on either side". Yet the battle established once for all British Power in India which continued to expand until the whole sub-continent came under its domination. No historian ever attempts to explain this miracle.

In contrast to the historian a scientist is concerned with some phenomenon, be it a social one. And as soon as he recognizes it he formulates a problem and it is this to which he devotes his attention. He attempts to confirm first, the reality of the phenomenon and then to discover the mechanism of action leading to that phenomenon. Only then he feels he has done justice to his subject. Applying such a two-step procedure to alchemy we start with the statement that gold was supposed to have been synthesized. Firstly the claim has to be confirmed and secondly the active principle which was powerful enough to change a base metal into gold. These two problems would be unavoidable in a proper presentation of alchemy, be it as pseudo-science.

Now there is no authentic record that gold was ever made. Prima facie there can be no history when there was no beginning. Then it would be a wonder how a bogus art could continue to persist for no less than several centuries. At least here some sort of explanation should be forthcoming. On the contrary I count myself among those who believe that alchemy, as actually started, still continues to exist, like a "living fossil" of culture, at least in India and Pakistan.

2. The agencies on which alchemy depended.

Granting alchemy's claim to be correct the problem further arises as to how gold was made; what were the actual substances and their active principles involved in the transformation of base metals. In Arabic there are two such substances, Kimiya and Iksir. Nothing corresponding exists in Greek. This sounds too bad to be true yet such absence can be confirmed. Taylor (1;66) admits that, "the principal feature that is lacking (in Greek Alchemy) is that of the elixir or the philosopher's stone". Even in Indian alchemy the word Rasayana by no means specifies an agent changing a base metal into gold. There are, however, others which would be mentioned later on. Since there can be no alchemy without such substances we presume that the same were nevertheless known to ancient workers in the field but we have overlooked the terms used by them. The blame would reasonably rest not with the original systems but with historians interpreting past records.

3. Other lacunae in the accounts of alchemy.

I have particularly emphasized the absence of

terms in Greek, corresponding to Kimiya and Iksir, for there can be no alchemy and thus no history of alchemy without them. Even otherwise there have been glaring omissions in the works of recognized authorities. Holmyard (2) has composed an otherwise excellent compendium entitled "Alchemy". It was independently reviewed by two reviewers. Prof. S. H. Nasr, writes in *Isis*, *1958*; 49:451, that "Holmyard's approach is basically historical rather than doctrinal, and it is through the passage of time rather than a unity of ideas that the book is organized and held together". The other critic was Prof. Hooykaas (3) who could not avoid noticing that "the one thing missing in the book is a clear exposition of alchemical theory". I fear this criticism applies to many treatises where we also miss the nature of the active agent responsible for transmutation of metals. Taylor's (1) own book, which is by no means inferior, contains not a word to explain the origin of the name alchemy without which its beginning remains unknown. Wilson (4), as its reviewer, missed this omission so much so that he tried to supply the etymology of the word as best as he could. Noticing other lacunae in the histories of alchemy Hopkins (5; p.v) was led to remark, as late as 1934, that, "the fundamental work of fact-finding was so time-consuming that no real history of alchemy has yet appeared". And the verdict was virtually extended to 1951, when Taylor (1; 16) confessed that, "it may at once be said that alchemy still remains an unsolved problem". Should my attitude appear hyper-critical, I admit that we nevertheless know more about Greek alchemy than that of any other. In fact we can interpret other systems best in terms of what is known of Greek alchemy. This is due to the indefatigable research of European and American scholars, to whom we are all grateful.

4. Cardinal points of knowledge.

To avoid any point unwittingly escaping our attention we must formulate a criterion and proceed with it stepwise. Its conditions would be those which carry full conviction. And they are nothing else than what may be called the cardinal points of knowledge. When translated as practical questions we would be required to know: 1. What was alchemy to begin with, and the same later on, 2. How was gold synthesized, the substances employed for it and their active principles, 3. Who founded it, and 4. Why. When we have answers to these inquiries we would automatically learn, 5. Where alchemy began, and 6. When. These six aspects of the history of alchemy are no less important than the six sides of a cube enabling us to perceive its solidity.

5. The positive criterion of alchemy as a whole.

We can further conceive criteria. external and internal, negative and positive, one serving as the background for the other in the foreground to appear in proper relief. For a positive criterion of a system of thought we cannot do better than look for an actual precedence. This is offered by De Ridder and Deonna (6) in their history of "Greek Art." It appears that, "the Doric building (as a work of art) is a unique whole. whose essential parts are logically to be deducted from one another". We may compare a whole to a family. There would be children and grandchildren and among themselves they would be as cousins of different degrees. The family pedigree has to be seen vertically and horizontally to realize it as a complete whole. It seems we can define a whole "as the integration of parts related among themselves as also to the whole". Such an integrated system, for example, is the human body of tissues and organs. As a corollary "if a part is ascribed to a whole it becomes directly or indirectly related to other parts" much as cousins do in a family. When the units multiply "parts remain mutually related and their integration expands as a complete whole". Then the parts are assigned their positions by their intrinsic virtues, the uses they reveal not to other parts, but to the whole. It is this emphasis on the whole which permits the constituents to be further interrelated among themselves. The make-up of the whole interests science and once it begins to exist as such its subsequent or obvious progress becomes the concern of history.

It is evident that no invention can be born without a preceding necessity. Discoveries by mere accidents are so rare as to be ignored; in fact even these come only to those who have been working to discover something else. Thus reasoning logically and considering chronologically the alchemist or the inventor must be assigned the first place and his invention or alchemy the second. The founder existed before alchemy and the motive with which he founded it implies some necessity or urge which he alone can best reveal. But if we now look into the histories of alchemy, they treat alchemy like a foundling picked up in some workshop at Alexandria. As such its parentage remains unknown and we know next to nothing of the very founder of the art. Nevertheless if the subject is to be presented as a whole the producer or the alchemist, deserves more attention than his product, or alchemy. In ignorance of its founder no history of alchemy can be forthcoming, a fact even otherwise recognized explicitly by Hopkins and implicitly by Taylor, both already cited.

6. Times that made alchemy.

It is true that men make times. But it is equally true that times make men. What then were the times which the founding members of alchemy actually had to face. This consideration takes us to the social history of those times. In proceeding thus we are further guided by Virchow (7), himself a maker of modern medical science. According to him "Medicine is a social science in its very bone and marrow".

And nothing better applies to alchemy which actually started as geriatrics, though conceived as the art of rejuvenation. Geriatrics is the real phase, rejuvenation its fabulous one, like chemistry and alchemy. Thus a realist would find geriatrics even where a pseudo-scientist claims it to be rejuvenation. It is the history of past social life which reveals how man really felt the need for rejuvenation and nothing short of it. Whether he achieved it is another story, but his urge was genuine and it made him an indefatigable seeker. Now much has been written on the history of medicine taking it to the earliest stage of civilization. Yet I do not know a chapter, much less a book, on the history of geriatrics, which thus raises a secondary problem for us. While we are looking at medicine as a discovery and an invention we are focussing attention on the social history representing the times that started medicine. This is but a phase of the same consideration which explains the evolution of species by environment forcing adaptation upon living forms. Pressure differing species became different. It means that environment makes species just as times make men. In accounting for the birth of any new form some necessity must be held as causal, thereby assuming the cause as emanating from the environment. Not only in biology but even in philosophy the same problem makes its importance felt. Thus Prof. S. H. Nasr (8) observes that, "one of the most important questions of Islamic philosophy (has been) the conditions under which some thing needs a cause". And the cause which led to the invention of alchemy rests entirely with the alchemist, its inventor. And we shall see that it was his urge for rejuvenation.

7. Social life created asceticism and this in turn an urge for rejuvenation.

In ancient times life's struggle was so severe that no form of social parasitism could be tolerated. To reduce the number of feeders infanticide of girls was practised. Women are not ideal bread-winners and less their number the better for the family. Likewise widows were burnt really to save others the trouble of supporting them. Next came the sick and the aged. Here Alberuni (9) writes that, in India during "most ancient times the bodies of the dead were exposed to the air being thrown in the fields without any covering (which is the case even today in rural parts of Tibet). Also sick people were exposed on the fields and in the mountains and left there. But if they recovered they returned to their dwellings". I have been informed of similar instances occurring in the interior of Sind. A temporary shed is constructed and chronic patients are left there to their fate and to the mercy of passers-by. Rarely they recover, usually they die, and are devoured by jackals. Peggs (10) cites typical instances of inclemency meted out to the infirm old parents not necessarily sick. Such people are taken to the bank of a river and left unattended. To expedite their death their mouths are filled with sand by their own children and their bodies pushed into the river thereby practising patricide. Thus speaks Peggs of Bengal of about 1800. At Rishikesh, a place of pilgrimage close to Hardwar and near Dehra Dun, India, there is a bridge over the Ganges. An infirm old father would be brought in a small Palki or palanquin, well garlanded, as befitting a pilgrim, and suddenly dropped into the river from over the bridge. Such cases though rare happen even today. We can now imagine how intolerant ancient times were towards the aged. In those days it was incumbent on every male member of the community to hunt together, fell forest trees and partake in tribal feuds. The aged were ill-suited for such strenuous duties and had to be eliminated. But here arose a difference according to the climatic conditions of the land.

If the aged belonged to a cold country like Germany, to exile him to a forest was to see him devoured overnight by a pack of hungry wolves. To avoid such a brutal death there arose a custom typical of heathenism. The old man was to be beheaded by his eldest son. He died as a hero to save himself the ignominy of a parasite and his family the burden of supporting an infirm. For accepting martyrdom, or willing death, he was promised Valhalla, the heaven of paganism.

But in a warm country like China or India, he could eke out an existence like a solitary deer of a forest. He was excommunicated to live like an outcast in a forest. Thus arose asceticism as an unavoidable social curse. It was confined to the aged, the male and to a warm country. The history of early asceticism, like that of geriatrics, has yet to be written; but I imagine it begins with civilization itself. At least when Buddha stepped out of his palace asceticism was fully recognized to welcome him.

This is admitted when Radhakrishnan (107; 97) states that, "retirement from the world is enjoined for every Aryan when once his duties to society are fulfilled". This is a polite way of saying, when he is superannuated.

Applying the theorem "that one essential part can be logically deduced from another" we shall see how facts accumulate to expand a consistent whole. Now the conditions of life, depicted above, which the aged exile had to face, created an immediate need to overcome the shock of solitude. Moreover he was to be his own grocer and cook, and had to collect food-stuffs in the form of vegetables and roots from all over the forest. He therefore needed strength enough to collect his daily ration. Thus he could not afford to neglect a single day for it would mean fasting. Any long sick leave would bring premature death from starvation, not to talk of inviting earlier some beasts of prey. Briefly, there arose two demands on the part of the old exile, immediately for an energizer and as soon as possible for a drug recalling the robust health of youth. To be able to remain physically fit, day after day, for an old man was nothing short of trying to become young again.

8. Birth of herbalism.

To find the proper place for geriatrics, or rather for the art of rejuvenation as it was actually conceived, we must have a picture of medicine as a whole. We are required to briefly recapitulate the history of early medicine. Man first treated himself by prayers. Words and sounds served like "invisible drugs". Thus arose "healing magic". Such a psychological system of treatment, starting as spiritual in nature, gradually became more and more material. With it the development, from using a common remedy, became more and more specific. Then plants also came to be used externally. Mere physical contact sufficed to bring about a cure. Vegetable products could even serve as charms or amulets. This became "herbal magic". The curative principle passed from a herb to the patient much as heat would. A plant was something like a magnet which by physical contact transfers its property to an inert piece of iron. Should this theory seem out of place to discuss, I beg to point out that it has survived to this day. Only when we recall such archaic ideas that we can interpret what persist as actual claims. There is a famous drug house manufacturing Eastern medicines and extols one of its preparations maintaining that, "the strength of the medicament passes into the system of the consumer". And what can diffuse unchanged from a plant into the human body. We know that vitamins should be able to pass as such in this way. But in ancient times Animism was the dominant system of thought. A plant, mineral and metal, each was a living entity and carried a soul. Soul could transmigrate and the strength of a medicinal plant was the quantum of soul it carried, which could be transferred into the system of the patient thereby conferring strength and curing him. Treatment was substitution therapy and the active principle was soul. To take a potion of herbal juice was to add to the stock of soul to a system running short of it. Man did not proceed at first from some abstract notion but empirically discovered the curative properties of plants and minerals. But such findings were rare and far between. Once Animism offered a theory be it ever so vague, evergreen plants, for example, were conceived as very rich in soul-content and thus more powerful than others, and a theoretical background was offered which gave rise to herbalism. Indeed nothing is more impressive than that Growth=Life, best exemplified by plants. Thus herbalism resulted from the impact of Animism upon empirical knowledge of plants, making "herbal soul" the active principle. Alchemy started as an offshoot of such herbalism; it produced herbo-metallic preparations, with soul from a plant as the active principle.

9. The first need of the ascetic for an energizer.

To be able to search for food-stuffs as forest produce the ascetic immediately needed an energizer. He had to cast off his depression and be on his legs to ransack the resources of the forest. The Aryan ascetic discovered the energizer as the plant Ephedra naming its juice Soma. Soma has been discussed and over-discussed making it more mysterious than before. Since we are dealing with the history of Indian alchemy it is but right that we first refer to the latest authority in the field who happens to be Prof. P. Ray (11). He writes that, "Soma (was) the *fermented juice* from the stems of some plant (not specified by him and) had been highly extolled and invoked as the representation of divine power." We can easily accept "divine power" as the virtue attributed to soul rather than to any material fraction of Soma. Reference to "fermented juice" implies the content to be alcoholic. Soma juice then would be an alcoholic drink.

Dhabar (12) discusses the same juice by its Iranian synonym, Haoma, and thereby quotes the "attributes of Bacchus", as follows : The liquid drink of grapes delivers the mortals from grief and gives sleep as an oblivion of daily evils; nor is there any other medicine for troubles". Thus alcohol was a tranquillizer and even sleep inducer. On the contrary, others, including the Aryan ascetics, found real energizers and these were non-alcoholic. Among the earlier writers who wished to know how Soma helped its Aryan users was Roth (13). He remarks that, "it is not quite clear what attributes must be assigned to the remarkable juice, Soma, (which) for the Aryans was what wine is for other people". Wine here passes merely as an anti-depressant whereas an energizer is far more. Trying to name the plant he could only refer to previous authors who imagined it to be *Asclepias acida*.

Now this herb cannot deliver a juice which can be fermented, nor is it anti-depressant in any way. Accordingly, later on Griffith (14) could correctly explain that, "the references to Soma as the god, the juice of the plant, and the moon, are very numerous. The plant was formerly supposed to be a milky climbing plant, *Asclepias acida*, it is now identified with a species of Ephedra, which in the Harirud Valley (in Baluchistan) is said to bear the name Hum, Huma and Yahma". These names would be variants of the Iranian word, Haoma, which is a synonym of Soma. The Iranians used the aspirant "H" for the Sanskrit sibilant "S", thereby equating Haoma=Soma. Griffith also translates a hymn from Atharva-Veda praying that, "the many plants that Soma rules asking (it to) deliver the suppliants from grief-and-woe"; and the life of the homeless old exile was full of them. If nothing else the food was not nourishing which alone could cause enough worries. Vishnu Purana, a holy scripture of the Hindus, as quoted by Ballantyne (15) informs that, "the anchorites live upon leaves, roots and (wild) fruits". The Indian ascetic was in no way better than the Greek sage, a sophisticated title for a pitiable ascetic, Heraclitus, who lived in Ionia, the warmer Asiatic Greece, and who, according to Enfield (16) "made choice of a mountainous retreat and lived upon natural produce of the earth. His diet and manner of life brought him dropsy." Thus, more than solitude, procurement of proper nourishment must have been a great source of "grief and woe" for the old ascetic. A sleeping draught or one amounting to the same, would not remove his shock, nor his hunger. He had to be active and he needed nothing other than an energizer, which would keep him alert, in full possession of his mental and physical powers, which had to be intensified because they were obviously weak for his life's struggle.

10. Comparative pharmacology of energizers.

Soma has been discussed without ever touching the active principle it actually contains. Even those who identified the Soma plant as Ephedra never went into the pharmacology of Ephedrine. As pointed out before, the homeless exile did not need a tranquillizer to forget his woes, but an energizer to help in his life's struggle. Now besides Ephedra there are two more herbs all as energizers. We first turn to a miner working in the cold and mountainous region of Peru and Bolivia. He works long, in the cold, without food and is poorly clad. He is hunger-proof and exhaustion-proof. The credit goes to the drug he uses. Lloyd (17) reports that the Incas labourers, belonging to that tribe of Red Indians, "become stronger, more satisfied and work all day without eating". For this "leaves are chewed which yield an abundance of vital strength". The plant is *Erythroxylon coca* which is "honoured in their sacred ceremonies by the recital, O ! Mighty Lord, let me recall the blessings of Divine Coca". Two phases logically serve as mirror images of each other, deification of the plant, as the positive and obvious, and drug-addiction, the prop of life, as the negative and obscure. Out of gratitude the Incas call Coca "the Divine Plant". This would naturally possess "Divine Power", such as P. Ray (11) has mentioned attributable to Soma.

A second energizer is *Catha edulis*, the Khat of Yemeni Arabs. According to Moser (18) like the Coca, here again "only fresh leaves are chewed". And as before with it a labourer "performs prodigies of strength and energy (while the drug also) exalts the spirits and supports bodily strength (and even) the gloomiest man becomes cheerful under its influence". In contrast to an intoxicant and a narcotic, an energizer, as Moser testifies, "after taking it myself late that night I was still awake".

Two properties suffice to look upon Ephedra as an energizer. First is its tendency to produce insomnia and Ephedrine is recognized to have such an effect. Second is its addiction and Panse and Klages (19) have shown Ephedrine to be a habit-former. As an energizer there is a hymn addressed to it in Atharva-Veda reproduced by P. Ray (11; 37). It prays that "the strength (soul) of this Amarita (Ambrosia) do we give this man to drink. Moreover I prepare a remedy that he may live a hundred years". It immediately confers strength, as an energizer would, and the feeling of well-being allows him to feel that the same drug can prolong life to a century or over. Moreover there is also an Iranian counterpart of the above hymn. Dhabar (12) reproduces it stating that, "Haoma is most nutritious for the soul, (being itself soul). It gives vigour of the entire frame". Thus Coca of Red Indians, Khat of Yemeni Arabs, and Soma of Aryan ascetics are all energizers, no intoxicants, nor narcotics, nor hallucinating drugs. For the actual benefits reaped, the Red Indian has made Coca the Divine-plant, the Yemeni Arab, who professing Islam could not deify a plant, has nevertheless made Khat the Flower of Paradise, and the Aryan ascetic, who enjoyed the most benefit, made Soma nothing short of a god. He had also made a god out of the cow so that a plant, which to the ascetic was the prop of his life, was more deserving of being deified. We must remember that such deifications occurred in times when man lived in close contact with nature and was mainly dependent upon it.

11. Soma as fresh plant juice and its herb.

The one feature which literary records can fully document makes Soma a freshly extracted plant juice, not one kept long to ferment. Its plant is an evergreen herb like the pine and its stems are also hard like pine-needles. They cannot be chewed or eaten but have to be pounded between stones and water used to facilitate complete extraction of the juice. Potions of freshly extracted juice were consumed and, although I missed such a record, I am convinced that it was taken daily. Then the plant must be such as to require the extraction of the juice by pounding its stems. Geldner, on pure literary evidence, concluded that it was Ephedra. The one source where all necessary information on the juice has been compiled is the thesis of Dr. Kapadia (20), a student of Prof. H. D. Velankar of Bombay, a renowned Indologist. It may be incidentally remarked that the treatment accorded to the stems of Ephedra would be quite different to that of a mushroom so that the juice extracted from the latter cannot be had in the manner described in Vedic literature. Now when a drug is accepted, as rejuvenating the aged, it automatically serves as that of resurrection. Immortality follows resurrection and eternal youth is a synonym of immortality. Thus once Ephedra was believed to rejuvenate it also served to revive the dead. Indeed Rig Veda which extols Soma as a drink of immortality contains a hymn, 10 : 57.3-4 maintaining that "the spirit of the dead man is called back to the dead body by Soma." Stein (21) accordingly found Ephedra interned with the dead in Central Asia, the last home of Aryans, and also found evidence to convince himself that the graves belonged to Aryan nomads. Stein further reports that a variant of the Iranian name Haoma also survived as Hum.

The living plant Ephedra has also been studied by Prof. Qazilbash (22) a botanist of Peshawar University. He also found a few variants of the names, Haoma and Soma, persisting in regions further north of Peshawar. Finaliy I (23) have been able to show that Ephedra has been carved on a Gandhara piece of sculpture now preserved in Archaeology Museum, Peshawar. The herb is being presented to Buddha by a herbalist. Buddha was not born an immortal, not being a deity. He therefore had to acquire immortality and would welcome a herb-of-immortality to remain as a drug-made-immortal. Thus Ephedra, as a drug of immortality, is depicted as being offered to him. As a plant Ephedra stems show joints comparable to those of a thin bamboo stem after being deprived of its leaves. This feature is too subtle to be carved on a small piece of stone. But Charaka (24; 496) refers to it as "the sovereign herb, which is known by the name Soma, (and) has fifteen *joints or knots* (per stem)". I believe no one has so far referred to Charaka's mention of the Soma plant.

With such details, collected by different workers, over a long period of scholarship, all pointing the Soma plant to be Ephedra, it comes as a surprise when Wasson (25) asserts that, Soma is the hallucinating mushroom, *Amanita muscaria.* Its properties are so prominent that had Soma been Amanita, the hallucinating powers would have been easily recorded in Vedic literature. Let us briefly compare another hallucinating mushroom. Irene Nicholson (26) mentions some Red Indian priests indulging in the use of such mushrooms. On p. 71 she writes that, "Dr. F. Guerra at Welcome Institute, London, working on the mushroom Teonanacatl, confirms its giving rise to a feeling of well-being but its enjoyment is followed by a deep sleep".

And the Aryan ascetic after collecting his ration from the forest had to cook before he could ever think of dosing. With Soma he could suffer from insomnia but with a mushroom he would be lulled to sleep on a hungry stomach. Finally Prof. Kashikar of Poona was kind enough to inform that Sir Harold Bailey (27) also identifies the Soma plant as a mushroom. His letter is dated 24th July 1973.

Had there been any mushroom as a drug of longevity-cum-immortality it would have certainly been mentioned in ancient Hindu literature. We shall see later that a number of herbal Rasayana preparations have been incorporated in the Codex of Charaka. A mushroom is conspicuous by its absence here as elsewhere. On the contrary the Chinese do record mushrooms as conferring longevity. Smith (28) mentions two such species, *Polyporus igniarius* and *P. lucidus*. About the latter he writes that, "it grows at the roots of trees. It lasts long when dried and can be recognized as an emblem of immortality". Its Chinese name is Ling-Chih or briefly Chih. Thus a mushroom has been mentioned in ancient Chinese literature. Had there been also one used by ancient Aryans either Iranian or Sanskrit records would have revealed the same. Moreover Amanita mushroom is not recognized even by Chinese Taoists.

12. The position of Rasayana in Indian medicine.

Just as we have considered the alchemist and his urge to found alchemy we wish to know the corresponding founder of medicine first. There can be only two sources of information on drugs, one accidentally discovered by many people and their findings gradually accumulating to form a system of medicine. The other would be the achievements of those who, for some reasons, made it their business to know medicinal plants. Here contribution to knowledge of medicine would be much greater. In this class come ascetics living like exiles in a forest and what they needed most was a drug of rejuvenation or at least one which could keep them strong and active enough to search for vegetable food-stuffs in a forest. They lived on the hopes of discovering a remedy for the infirmity of old age. Searching for the impossible they came to discover the properties of so many herbs that they unwittingly became the founders of herbalism which was the original medicinal system both of India and of China. And this is shown by the stamp they have clearly left on the character at least of Indian medicine. Medical science is called Ayurveda. Literally it means science of life or biology. Then a science concerned with life must also look to the preservation of life and thereby to curing ailments; hence Ayurveda signifies medicine. The actual drugs are called Aushadhs, a word derived from a root meaning plant, since in the beginning most medicines were herbs. As distinct from the art of treating diseases, there also existed the art of rejuvenating the aged and this was named Rasayana. It has been explained above that the latter was the primary concern of the ascetic who only incidentally came to discover remedies for other diseases to which he himself must have been subjected. Social history of the times clearly makes the ascetic first a seeker of rejuvenation and next and incidentally the seeker of cures for diseases. This presumably was the state already in Rig Vedic times. Atharva-Veda which came later, and as echo of earlier times, contains hymns of two kinds clearly pointed out by Sir P.C. Ray (29; p. VIII). "One is called Bhaishajyani for curing diseases and driving away demons (which in those days were supposed to cause ailments). The other had for its object the securing of long life and health (and) is known as Ayushyani, a term which later on gave place to Rasayana, the Sanskrit equivalent of alchemy". Following him both Prof. P. Ray (11) and Prof. N.R. Dhar(30)have stated the same almost using his very words.

Then to believers in spirits, just as a tyrant may enslave a man depriving him of his freedom, a diabolic spirit can overpower a man when he loses his health. Thus as far as diseases are concerned they all have an external etiology. But old age is no disease. Here to aspire for longevity is to maintain all intrinsic assets as such. However these are being regularly depleted and youth departs without promising to return. Then there is no other option than to restart life, as it were, from a scratch, to be born again, just as a serpent does when he moults regularly from year to year. Health is restored by driving away a foreign spirit but youth is restored by repeating birth which means repeating creation. Here the entire constitution is to be reconditioned, by an all-changing agency. The earliest way of achieving longevity, implying rejuvenation, was by performing Ayushyani prayers. Now just as there is "poetic licence" we can acquire an "interpreter's licence". Using such a prerogative we interpret Ayurveda or medicine proper as the descendant of its progenitor, the Bhaishajyani prayers in Atharva-Veda; and Rasayana, the art of rejuvenation or geriatrics, as that of the Ayushyani prayers. This word has been translated by Monier-Williams (31) as "giving long life", but one can be justified in interpreting it as "immortal life," which however implies a previously existing notion of "eternal youth" which is the stage after one has accepted rejuvenation first. Instead of taking Rasayana or rejuvenator to some prayers, as "invisible drugs", I take it to a definite herb, Ephedra, which is Soma, an energizer. Thereby the origin of Rasayana is virtually taken to pre-Atharva-Veda period, to that of Rig Veda. I believe it is even older for we cannot overlook legends which have survived even to this day. We must know when begins the idea of rejuvenation. With whom it begins is clear by now, it is the ascetic, but asceticism seems to be a product at least of the forest civilizations of India and China.

13. Prehistoric cosmogony supporting the idea of rejuvenation.

We can arbitrarily divide Indian medicine into three periods, pre-Vedic, Vedic and post-Vedic, the last being a synonym of the earliest stage of codified medicine. In the earliest cosmogony the first element to have existed is water. Water created the universe and it also created life. This idea was widely spread literally from China to Peru. Rig Veda recognizes it. The Holy Quran, 30 : 21, also states that "Life was created in water". When water created life, water can best preserve life. Moving waters specially possessed therapeutic properties, above all warm springs with their mysterious heat and a more mysterious terrestrial origin. Even New Testament refers to a chronic patient waiting to be cured by entering as the first into the floods of a spring. Such "baths" all over the world, including the one near Karachi, have a very long past. Even Baptism can be traced to the spiritual healing powers of water, originally of "moving water" of a brook rather than of a lake, best of a river like Ganges. Thus such waters could rejuvenate the old and there arose "fountains or springs of eternal youth". On the contrary there never was a "lake of eternal youth", with stagnant water.

Next came herbs growing in deep waters conferring rejuvenation and ever-lasting youth. To its later period belong preparations like Amarita in Sanskrit and Ambrosia in Greek. These words have a common Aryan root implying that the Greeks and Hindus had accepted the idea when they lived together in Central Asia, the home of the Aryan peoples before they separated themselves. Amarita and Ambrosia are drugs of immortality which is the most effective form of saying that they are also drugs of rejuvenation. I need not continue to identify these two virtues in later discussions. Then Amarita—Ambrosia are legendary drugs which merely mean that we have no record of their long past but can nevertheless be looked upon as the bygone ancestors of Rasayana preparations. All through a lineal descent there has been the recurring motive of rejuvenation. In Vedic times we have Soma as the drug of rejuvenation-cum-immortality. Since Iranians profess the same veneration for Soma calling it Haoma its use was already pre-Vedic when Hindus and Iranians lived together. We finally come to post-Vedic period which is assumed here to begin with Charaka. He is to Indian medicine what Hippocrates is to that of Greece. We are now in historical times and interpretations can be documented.

14. Charaka and his two categories of medicines.

Sir P. C. Ray (29; XIII) assigns Charaka a much earlier date than does the French savant Sylvan Levi. The latter makes him "the court physician of the Indo—Scythian king, Kanishka, who reigned in the 2nd Cent. A.D.". Prof. Sufi (32) writing in 1949 seems to agree with Levi. I am interested in a practising physician who is also the first to codify medicine in India. As such Levi's theory appeals at least as an expediency measure not likely to be improved upon. P. C. Ray (29; 32) quotes Charaka defining Rasayana as follows : "Medicines are of two kinds, the one promotes the strength and vitality; the other cures diseases. Whatever promotes longevity, health and virility is called Rasayana". We note that priority is assigned to Rasayana which represents drugs of rejuvenation. Strange enough, medicines proper, curing diseases, come next in rank. Nothing corresponding can be found in any other system of medicine, certainly not in the Codex of Hippocrates. This preference for Rasayana is traceable to the ascetic who went out searching for medicinal plants, not to cure ailments, but to rejuvenate himself. And it is the same ascetic who recited the two kinds of hymns recorded in Atharva-Veda. One prayer is called Bhaishajyani, for curing diseases, and the other Ayushyani, interpreted properly as desiring rejuvenation-cum-longevity. The two prayers in Atharva-Veda then correspond to the two divisions of medicine, Ayurveda proper and Rasayana. Thus he who recited Bhaishajyani hymns gave his thoughts a material form and established Ayurveda or medicine proper, and the reciter of Ayushyani hymns correspondingly founded Rasayana or the art of geriatrics-cum-rejuvenation which the founder needed personally.

By now Charaka's Codex (24) has been translated and annotated in six large volumes. In vol. V a chapter begins (on p.473) recognizing only "two kinds of medicines, one as promotive of vigour in the healthy, the other destructive of disease in the ailing". The former division is called Rasayana. It is not to be mistaken with aphrodisiacs for which the term used is Vajikarana (p.474). Aphrodisiacs can be legitimately required even by the debilitated young and are actually used mostly by such young people who wish to fully enjoy sexual life. Rasayanas on the contrary were specific remedies for rejuvenation and as such meant for the aged, if they otherwise were free from any disease. The drugs were so powerful that they could also treat incurable diseases. The active principle was soul, an entity which is all-growing and all-changing. By its use no tissue, gland or organ, can remain indolent and all were forced to function normally. This would see that the aged loses his wrinkles and even the seriously ill his paleness. Charaka as the compiler of what he found well-recognized could not but assign priority to such wonderful preparations; moreover he seems to have been convinced for he offers his own recipes.

15. Herbal Rasayanas.

The foremost among the Rasayanas, in Charaka, comes "Cyavana Prasa" Linctus (24; 478). It was conceived and tried upon himself by the sage Cyavana. It is celebrated as the highest Rasayana.

"By its use Cyavana though grown very old became young once again. By recourse to this vitalization the great sages, such as Cyavana and others, regained their youth, became most attractive to women and acquired the capacity to *bear all hardships*", an indispensable asset for the lonely ascetic (pp.481-482). Charaka gives a long recipe of Cyavana's preparation with all ingredients as herbal. The major item is Amala, *Phyllanthus emblica*, next the myrobalan, *Terminalia chebula* or Harr. Now Amala is the richest natural source of ascorbic acid, or vitamin C. This can reduce yellow gold chloride to red colloidal gold even in a cold solution. The other myrobalan is rich in tannins which can reduce gold chloride in a boiling solution. Thus both the above drugs are strong reducing substances. Lastly Ghee or boiled butter is used as the preserving vehicle along with honey which again has reducing properties.

The three drugs *Phyllanthus emblica*, Amala; *Terminalia chebula*, Harr; and *T. belerica*, Bahera are called "tirphala", three-fruits, and it is translated into English as "three-myrobalans". It is Arabicized as Atrifal. Charaka (p. 480) gives a preparation with the three-myrobalans as the main constituent. But this is further saturated with Ghee or boiled butter which must be looked upon as the fourth component of the preparation. This emphasis on Ghee is best confirmed in the light of another preparation, designated as the "Emblic myrobalan Ghee" (p.482) and it is claimed that its user "remains young for a hundred years and acquires unimpaired sex-vigour and becomes the parent of many children". Here I cannot help recalling the latest work on longevity by Prof. D. Harmann (33) of Nebraska. He found "anti-oxidants increase the life-span of mice by 44 p. c. And when the results on animals are converted to human terms the life-span of man would increase from 70 to 100 years". Harmann found oil-soluble anti-oxidants to be effective; he also tried ascorbic acid but with indifferent results. Charaka however emphasizes the use of both, water-soluble ascorbic acid and Ghee, which would contain its own oil-soluble anti-oxidant. He thus unwittingly realized such importance, for, on p.503, he mentions "the virilific Ghee", where boiled butter is the main constituent of that Rasayana.

Remembering that "one essential feature is logically deduced from another", if Amala and Soma are both drugs of longevity we expect other common extra medicinal uses. Soma plant was used to furnish a drink of immortality; it was used also as the agency of resurrection to be interned with the dead. With virtues bestowed upon Amala as rejuvenating the aged, we expect it to find its secondary use as a drug-of-immortality. All this follows logically from the assumption that Amala carried a rich quantum of soul next only to Soma or Ephedra. Dikshit (34; 63) carried out excavations at Ahichchatra, a famous site in India. There he found "Amala shaped beads of faience with traces of high green glaze", and Amala is a yellowish - green fruit. These beads are dated prior to 350 A. D. Then he further mentions, "Amalaka shaped terracotta dark brown colour well fired" beads of about 200 A. D., and Amala on drying becomes dark brown. These beads would be of the same age in which Charaka is supposed to have lived. Lal (35; plate LVI) also found at Hastinapura, Meerut Distt., beads which he illustrates as resembling the natural Amala fruit even better. His findings are dated 100 B. C. - 200 A. D. The beads were worn as charms which would be expected to offer longevity, if nothing more. Archaeologists further mention that Amala has also served as the model for architectural domes. I find its six concave sided seed has been projected to shape such a dome in one of the temples in Ellora caves, near Aurangabad, India. That Amala was venerated to the extent of donating its shape to temple architecture is expected from its having been recognized as conferring immortality. Only Amala has not been deified since its discovery came apparently later than Vedic times.

16. Metallic preparations as Rasayana.

I have devoted much time conceiving the oxidation-reduction system of the aged as compared with that of a youth. This is most vital for understanding geriatrics. Here I can recall a simple phenomenon explained by Friend (36). He writes that, "in 1740 cast-iron guns from a Spanish ship sunk off the coast of Mull had lain in the sea for 152 years. On scrapping away the corroded surface they became hot to touch. Iron had undergone reduction to ferrous oxide which on coming into contact with the oxygen of the air rapidly oxidized to ferric oxide with the evolution of heat, the reaction being strongly exothermic". This phenomenon, though belonging to the inorganic world, can serve as a model to elucidate the difference between the biological systems of the old and the young. The item of primary importance is a reducible substance. It is this which, on contact with air, delivers energy as heat. But heat is only one form of energy; the same reduced substance can offer other forms which can not be discussed here. We accept the proverbial recognition of the aged as having a cold body whereas the young a warm one. But what the system of the aged lacks are reducing substances; ascorbic acid would be one, oil-soluble antioxidants would be another. Thus the genesis of warmth characterizing the robust health of youth is traced to the presence of reducing substances. Here reduced iron would be a third, by no means less important than the other two. Iron is the decisive constituent of blood, responsible for its role of respiration and body temperature. We therefore assume that iron is not recurringly reduced in the body of an old man from want of reducing substances. Then what is not utilized is excreted and we otherwise know that old people look anaemic from want of enough iron and thus of enough haemoglobin in the system. But it is also obvious that if depleted stock of iron is to be replaced reducing substances have also to be supplemented; iron which cannot be reduced is no iron and would be excreted. And we also find specialists in geriatrics wisely recommending both iron and ascorbic acid. Here Charaka rightly assigns first place to Amala, which is rich in vitamin C.

That he has not overlooked iron now draws our attention. Charaka (on p. 489) has an "Iron Vitalizer". Its method of preparation would now be called as that of "calcined metals". This term serves as the designation of metallic preparations, called "Kushtas", literally "Killed" metals, in Persian, and "Bhasmas", meaning killed by being "burnt", in Sanskrit. And their methods of preparation are typical of alchemy. Charaka recommends iron to be beaten into thin plates, then heated red-hot in fire, dipped in reducing agents, above all in extract of Amala, then pulverized and finally preserved in Amala extract, and honey, with its own reducing sugars. It is left in an earthen vessel for over a year which would thoroughly reduce iron to a ferrous compound. The preparation is to be taken with "honey and Ghee every morning" (p. 490). If continued for a year one will acquire "the vitality of an elephant" and become "immune to disease, old age and to death". Such would be "calcined iron" or Iron-Rasayana, herbo-ferrous or herbo-metallic in its make-up.

Storing for a year would guarantee iron as completely reduced. Here we can look for two interpretations, one of a natural phenomenon similar to the one which Friend offers and another which the alchemist would.

17. Charaka extolling Iron and a reducing agent.

Another vitalizer is called "the Brahma vitalizer" containing Emblic myrobalans *(P. emblica)* and Iron.

This declaration of its contents pinpoints two ingredients, ascorbic acid and iron. It emphasizes the importance of the two drugs in geriatrics, which can be fully endorsed by modern medicine. Charaka extols it saying that, it is "Capable of keeping a man alive for thousand years (being) invented by Brahma, the Creator himself". It is not yet obvious to which of the two Charaka would impart priority. However, no vitalizer is purely metallic nor is iron calcined by itself. On the contrary he has a "Simple Emblic myrobalan vitalizer" (p. 489) and explaining it he writes that, "as many fruits (of Amala) as he eats so many millenniums does he live with youth restored. Eating to his fill of such fruits he becomes like unto the gods". He would have otherwise called Amala, the Divine Fruit, since the recommendation comes from Brahma, the Creator. We have here to realize the style in which the ancient thinkers used to express themselves. If a Red Indian found Coca to be the Divine Plant, Charaka found Amala to have been prescribed by Brahma, the Creator, making its user god-like, by which is meant young and immortal. All gods in Greek and Hindu religions are models of young people. This makes a deity or a god a synonym of "eternal youth".

18. Charaka's incidental mention of a gold preparation.

Charaka's paragraph on Iron Vitalizer ends by stating that, "in the same manner the use of other metals such as gold and silver is promotive of longevity and a tried panacea". We can definitely conceive the gold preparation as herbo-aurous or herbo-metallic for calcination is always accompanied by a herbal principle and further pulverization is facilitated by the use of herbal extracts, fresh or as decoction. Had alchemy existed in Charaka's time he would have at least given priority to gold over iron. On the contrary, to him as a physician, gold rightly comes far behind iron. He gives the reader the impression that he tried to make his Codex exhaustive, leaving no trace element without some mention. In an earlier communication I (37) have explained how such a herbo-aurous preparation can be made by a most primitive method. Gold is granulated and rubbed in a granite mortar and pestle with herbal extracts, preferably of Amala and myrobalans, which Charaka recommends. When the process is continued, be it for a few months, yellow gold becomes a brick-red powder. When further pulverization does not increase the shade of redness the preparation is pronounced to be perfect. Here we can legitimately affirm to the effect that which transformed yellow gold into a red metallic powder was a herb or better still its juice. We know otherwise that the reducing substances of a plant can turn yellow gold into its red colloidal form. The juice then can be reasonably designated as the red-gold-making juice or simply gold-making juice. The importance of this term would be realized later on. It is to be noted that even though no calcination was employed gold was pulverized with herbal principles. The explanation is that pulverization or rubbing promotes colloidal formation. This is greatly accelerated by adding reducing agents coming from plants. To the Animist however pulverization was killing the metal with physical force and using a herbal principle was resurrecting it by infusing a herbal soul. It produced a Resurrection Body.

19. Silajit or mineral pitch vitalizer.

In Charaka, as vitalizers, first come pure herbal preparations and next herbo-metallic, usually called "calcined metals". Thirdly (on p. 493) there is a "mineral pitch" vitalizer, and we shall see that by its make-up it is herbo-mineral. This pitch is called today Silajit. Charaka informs that it is "exuded by mountain rocks loaded with gold and other metallic ores; all varieties of which have the smell of cow's urine". A genuine sample of Silajit was brought for me by an archaeologist friend from Chitral, up north in Pakistan. It looked like a rock consisting of sand and pebbles cemented with some pitch which however was not obvious. This became at once evident when the rock was easily dissolved in water producing a solution dark brown in colour resembling humus. I gave a piece of the dry rock to my son, Irfan, to smell when he was not yet 10. As a child he was fond of animals and knew the cow and goat well. Yet he took no time to declare that the rock smells of horse. Silajit contains hippuric acid and the word was so coined because horse-urine contains it. In fact urine of all herbivorous animals contains hippuric acid and as such also of the cow. Cow's urine was used in several rituals, both by ancient Iranians and Hindus, which explains Charaka's familiarity with it and his comparison of the smell of Silajit with cow's urine. The origin of Silajit has not been investigated. Just as coal represents plants buried in mines, decomposed vegetation buried as rock is Silajit. Such would be the provisional account of its origin. Charaka extols it as being loaded with minerals like gold. I submitted a portion of the Silajit I had to an American Chemist who kindly reported the presence of several trace elements, silver being one, but no gold. Thus there is some evidence to support Charaka's claims. We know that trace elements are constituents of different enzymes and Silajit, as supplying them, would be of great therapeutic value. Trying to close this paragraph we note that even Silajit is herbal in origin and is therefore a herbo-mineral, though a natural product. The importance of a herbal principle has remained constant and only in this light we can appreciate how Silajit has also been extolled as a panacea. But whereas herbal-Rasayanas and herbo-mineral Rasayanas are natural products, herbo-metallic Rasayanas were not found in nature and alchemy made it its concern to make them. Thus started alchemy, as pharmaceutical chemistry, retaining the objective of rejuvenation. It must not be overlooked that in

Charaka no mercurial is mentioned, whereas cinnabar was the drug of choice among the Chinese and its synthetic preparation, as vermilion, gave rise to alchemy which at its beginning was only concerned with rejuvenation.

20. Calcined metals as Phlogiston.

We have discussed why Charaka recommends storing his iron-preparation for a year to mature it. It implies reduction identical with what Friend described of submerged iron guns producing ferrous oxide. Davis (38 ; 332), discussing theoretical alchemy observes that, "Stahl's discovery was that combustibility is transferable. We would now say the material which results from a reduction is itself capable of acting as a reducing agent. He gave the name of Phlogiston". Then "reduced iron" was prepared so as to serve as a "reducing agent" which can be designated Phlogiston. And the iron vitalizers of Charaka would be such Phlogistons, a very important conclusion. Moreover all anti-oxidants would become valuable as geriatric drugs.

21. Calcined metals as alchemical preparations.

The explanation equating Rasayana=Phlogiston is quasi-alchemical. We proceed further to appreciate what a genuine alchemist would have to say. Here we begin by referring to an excellent article by Sampson (39; 491). He writes that, "Paracelsus accepted the doctrine of the alchemists that a bird after being burnt could be restored to life by the putrefaction (=incubation) in a sealed vessel". We shall first handle putrefaction and then the rebirth of the bird which was burnt to death. In Charaka the iron-Amala preparation was kept in an earthen pot for one whole year. Hermetical sealing was unknown to him which was first conceived by the Chinese as I (40) have explained elsewhere. That Charaka emphasizes long storage for maturation can be easily accepted as the incubation of his preparation. Friend's observation on iron guns under sea also comes under this category of "incubation" prior to iron being reduced to ferrous oxide. We now wish to interpret this reduction of iron as an alchemist would.

Our term incubation is a synonym of the alchemist's putrefaction. Incubation refers to time or to temperature, or to both, and to nothing more. Putrefaction however signifies post-mortem dissolution of corporeal elements. A rotten egg for example will show its contents having undergone putrefaction. Thus putrefaction follows death. Here comes the special interpretation of the phenomenon by the alchemist. An egg which is rotten has suffered death, but an egg revealing incubation has undergone so to say pseudo-death. It is the end of one stage and beginning of another. A chicken can be conceived as having three periods in its life cycle, one of latency of growth, as in the fresh egg, then of proper growth as embryo still in the egg, initiating dissolution of previous contents and reshuffling the morphological elements thus produced to finally reconstruct a living form. Let us consider an old house being replaced by new architecture. The building will be demolished into broken walls which cannot be utilized for reconstruction. The walls will be further reduced to debris of stones and bricks which then can be duly exploited. Putrefaction or incubation brings the contents of the egg to a stage comparable not to broken walls but to stones and bricks. If these be further dissolved only then in one case the egg will become rotten, and in the other sand and dust as perfect ruins. Thus putrefaction depicts an earlier stage than the last, as the development of inert life into dynamic life, of a shapeless mass into elements capable of reconstruction. A seed during germination shows corresponding putrefaction or dissolution of previous parts into a plastic mass which enables reshaping, with growth generated thereby, into an impressive living whole. The fact not to be overlooked is that putrefaction is internal or submerged growth. This remains undetected in the beginning when no growth is obvious. But it serves as the maker of plastic mass which ultimately shapes a chicken. Thus when the end result is a living chick and its previous state can be described as "putrefaction of the egg" this can only be growth undetected as many a phenomenon in nature is. Putrefaction, judged by what actually follows it, is growth. Putrefaction can be best compared with fermentation where again growth is energetic yet unobservable. Briefly, putrefaction is growth starting with dissolution of previous elements and re-synthesis of micro-elements into macro-fractions, then into tissues and organs which develop as a whole into a chicken. It is destruction leading to new reconstruction. It is a kind of reshuffling.

To the alchemist, as Animist, even a metal had life but ordinary iron was "dead metal", while reduced iron oxide generating heat on contacting air, would be a "live mineral". He thus took inert raw materials and tried to infuse life into them and once they became living entities they could transfer their life-essence on to man and prolong his life. Inert materials carried life, as does an egg. They were potentially living and alchemy, as art, tried to convert what is potential into a dynamic form. Moreover it was not to be any soul or a rich quantum of it, it was to be an ever-increasing soul, qualitatively superior to those of any simple, or individual drug, be it Soma plant or metal-gold. And this requires evacuating the unstable soul and replacing it by an ever-growing one which alone is ever-lasting. In effect it means killing and resurrecting. Here the vehicle or the body is to be retained and the life-prolonging element alone is to be substituted. Thus there is no immortality without resurrection or rebirth as in the legend of Phoenix.

22. The legend of the Phoenix as implying resurrection.

This legend easily explains the theory of resurrection and also of alchemy which tries to imitate resurrection. The bird flapped its wings against the dried twigs of its nest. The friction generated heat and produced fire. The bird was burnt but was reborn. This legend transferred to alchemy gives a correct picture of calcined metals or metallic Rasayanas. To begin with, if the bird was burnt to death, a Rasayana is actually called today Bhasma. or the "burnt one", and in Persian, "Kushta", the "killed one". And killing or death is the necessary prelude to resurrection. "The dead one" becomes the first stage for the next to be "the resurrected one". Phoenix was an ordinary mortal bird, but after being burnt, the vegetable principle, latent in the twigs of its nest, revived it, now making it immortal. The right emphasis is on its immortality. Now there is a Chinese legend, same as the story of the Phoenix. A prince of Hui Nan (41) took an elixir of life which his dog and a cock also picked up as residues and ultimately all died. But subsequently the three revived and became drug-made-immortals. Their "mortal soul" was replaced by an "immortal soul" generated by the drug. Phoenix was the designation of a "resurrected bird" which is but synonym of an "immortal bird". The prince of Hui Nan, who had a parallel career, became Hsien-Shen, a designation for a drug-made-immortal. He was first killed, his elements of mortality sponged out, and reconditioned to enable him to remain young for ever. The change took place in the material nature of the flesh. It became soul-like and the body now "Resurrection Body", which Schep (42) has beautifully described as the original body of Jesus revealing super-material or sublime properties. With such a body Jesus could reveal super-human virtues. After his resurrection Jesus could be seen all over as though space did not exist. Finally he ascended to Heaven and so did the prince of Hui Nan in broad day light (41). As we are referring to Jesus, we realize his three days in the grave as what "putrefaction" would be in the eyes of the alchemist, or "incubation" when the mortal remains are being reconditioned to become immortal. Matter or flesh was not decomposed but gained spiritual properties. Resurrection Body was not a "gaseous body" but the original body of Jesus, highly spiritualized. When iron becomes magnetized, it remains iron but becomes a super-metal and correspondingly the material body of Resurrection Body becomes soul-like. There was no sense in changing the body and thereby the individual. The entire idea started with preserving the body itself and only losing its infirmities. To change the body was to become another individual, it would be reincarnation, the body being new, the soul remaining as before. On the contrary resurrection retains the body and allows a soul to revive it. Then alchemy imitates resurrection which in some cases becomes identical with reincarnation but this is incidental. Applying the idea of resurrection to the preparation of medicaments, "calcined metals" become products of burnt-and-resurrected metals, or herbo-metallic, where the metal was killed by heat, and the soul coming from a herb resurrected it and made it ever-lasting. The history of such a preparation follows three stages of resurrection: death, "incubation", and rebirth. In this paragraph "incubation" has been explained as submerged growth or putrefaction.

23. Growth versus Reproduction.

We have said earlier that growth is life. It is an axiom implying definition of life. Then to grow is to be alive. Since crystals of minerals grow, Animism considers minerals to be living entities. Even well-shaped metals, as distinct from rust, are endowed with soul and life. This can be confirmed by the belief that metals are supposed to grow. Friend (36;18) writes that, the "Tibetan gold miners collect and export gold dust; they refuse to touch the nuggets as they are believed to breed the dust. In fact the nuggets are the geese that lay the golden eggs". Here increment may result from expansion or vegetative growth of crystals which can crumble into dust, be it of gold. Or the crystals can breed or reproduce which can hardly apply to the case above. Friend has mistaken increment by growth for increment by reproduction. Usually no such subtle difference is made and this only makes our case difficult to explain. The Tibetans are Animists and Animism is a generalization and abstraction of the phenomenon of growth. It is Dualism that is correspondingly based on reproduction.

We are particularly interested in the origin of that growth which starts with incubation. Obviously before incubation there was perfect latency and what appeared later as putrefaction, like fermentation, was growth of some kind. We have here a dynamite, as it were, which needs a little external heat to explode as growth. Incubation thus is a condition, whereas putrefaction is the resultant growth. As a typical case of condition, distinct from a genuine cause, we can consider the following one. Frogs do not die of typhoid. But when a frog is inoculated and incubated the germ is provided with the temperature necessary for its multiplication and such a frog succumbs to the disease. It is otherwise immune because it is a cold-blooded creature and the typhoid germ does not multiply at low temperatures. Thus a condition of life being provided converts latency of life into its dynamic form, nothing really being added to it. The axiom further maintains that wherever there is a form of life, it is alive and there is potential growth. A plant, a crystal, and a metal, all have specific forms, and all are endowed with a life-essence, their quanta however differing considerably. Having arrived at this stage of clarity we can appreciate Sampson (39; 490) informing that, "the Archaeus, a personification of life-force in all created things (possessing specific forms) was invented by Paracelsus and discussed by van Helmont to elucidate the putative volitional power of matter to grow, to resist disease, to heal and to reproduce itself". And "Archaeus was nothing else than seminal power of every seed". Previous thinkers have mixed the doctrines of Animism and Dualism or rather traced total increment to growth and reproduction without assigning due share to each. When a flock increases it is due to reproduction whereas when a creeper spreads out, like a carpet, it is due to growth. But when a plant grows the cells of its tissues multiply. Nevertheless we do recognize that an ovum, or egg can grow from a negligible size to an appreciably large one and there the growth stops. Once it is fertilized and later incubated, cells multiply and these shape themselves into a living form. Thus future life starts with the union of opposites and incubation is a condition incidental to the cause. A self-growing entity becomes reproductive when it is made up of two opposites. It is like magnetism arising with a magnet or a piece of iron with two poles, without which there is no magnetism. Our position would not be clear unless we admit first, conditions of life, e.g. temperature in the case of typhoid bacteria changing their potentiality of growth into actual dynamic growth which really means life. Then the nature of soul or life-essence is inherent in its vehicle. It must be dual-natured to be able to grow and multiply, like two digits which may be added or may be multiplied according to circumstances. Animism, with a mono-elemental soul, could not explain any origin, because such a soul could only go on repeating or adding what there was to begin with. With two sub-souls, the resultant can become multiplicative which far surpasses the starting material. We then mistake the product as though something marvellous has resulted. What becomes multiplicative or reproductive we call creative because it becomes impressive. But just as growth in essence is addition, reproduction in essence is multiplication. Such a separation of dual forces supporting life can be expressed in old terminology as due to two sub-souls as distinct from a soul which is mono-elemental. In an earlier article I (43) have called the two fractions of soul, Growth-soul and Soul-reproductive, thus linking biology with mysticism. Growth-soul is a connotative name for growth-inducing power which even to biology is a mystery. Likewise we do not know what sets a fertilized cell to start self-division. Thus can be conveniently designated Soul-reproductive, the actual origin of the phenomenon of reproduction or multiplication, subsequent to maximum growth, remaining again a mystery in biology. Moreover identifying Growth-soul with Brahman of Indian mysticism and Soul-reproductive with Atman, is again the main problem of Indian philosophy. We would be excused, when on facing the same problem in theoretical alchemy, we cannot make the reader wiser than before. But what has been done here is a study of comparative general philosophy including theoretical alchemy and Indian philosophy, as schools of Dualism and Monism. Finally we must admit that Life = Growth + Reproduction and if Soul = Life-essence then Soul = Growth-soul + Soul-reproductive. This enables us to understand at once how Paracelsus speaks of "Archaeus as seminal power of every seed". His "Seminal power" is the sub-soul, called here Soul-reproductive. A seed grows but has the potentiality to reveal reproductivity when required. Perhaps both, growth and reproduction, operate together at every stage, only reproduction becomes obvious after the plant is full grown. Reproduction seems to be transcendent growth.

24. Growth intrinsic to matter.

If we face reproduction first it can be traced back

to growth. What then is its origin. It practically means what is the origin of matter itself. We start with some primordial energy. A quantum of energy freezes and becomes matter as a shell with a trace of energy remaining at its core. No matter is free from energy. The creation or matter carries its "creator" or energy. The Upanishads have described this phenomenon stating that the creator created the Universe and then entered into it. The two explanations are identical. Then matter is also the carrier of energy and the latter, as the progenitor, is what Paracelsus calls "life-force in all created things." Energy tends to expand but enclosed in matter forces the latter to grow as much as it can. This explains "the power of matter to grow" to which Paracelsus refers. If the quantum of energy is limited, or relatively the enveloping matter excessive, growth becomes slow. On the contrary if there is much energy, within a mere shell of matter covering it, growth will explode the shell and further reconstructions and rebirths of matter can occur. But also imagine two units of matter each with "power to grow". Their union would result in reproduction. Dualism however suggests that it is not merely two kinds of matter but exact opposites. I further identify the opposites as mirror images which can easily be taken to a common source like Adam and Eve to the same clod of earth. Here the Upanishadic account is even better; it takes creation to a two-seeded fruit. When matter, with its inherent energy expands, it results in the break-up of the entity. But when two such units of matter, further qualified as opposites, unite they do not grow to destroy each other but mutual growth results in division which is reproduction. A fertilized egg is bi-elemental, incorporating two centres of potential growth. Incubation is a mere condition promoting growth in this case of the dual-natured egg. The resultant growth of opposites with interactions upon each other results in shaping a self-supporting independent life-form, be it as a chicken.

25. Animism versus Dualism.

To fully appreciate alchemy we must understand both Animism and Dualism, which in turn are traceable to man's conceptions of Growth and Reproduction respectively. Its importance is at once realized when we take "Putrefaction" of the alchemist as due to the "life-force in all created things" and further down to "the power of matter to grow". Since we have just explained Growth and Reproduction, we can turn to Animism and Dualism. The idea of Soul starts with Animism. Man by nature is indifferent to such an abstruse problem. But the conception was forced upon man even when he was a hunter. He killed game but also wild beasts and his enemies. A wounded wolf for example was still a danger and to distinguish the living and the dead he had to conceive the nature of life-essence. Since most deaths which he observed occurred from loss of blood, the formula of life became Life=Body+blood and Blood=Soul, as mono-elemental. And we still believe: Life=Body+Soul. When the primitive thinker came to inquire into the nature of a mineral or what it consists of he explained it in terms of human constitution. Even a mineral was made up of a body and soul. This doctrine is called Animism. A stone also dies and becomes dust. But Animism could not explain origin of things, not even human birth properly. There still exist tribes in Australia and Melanesia on which Malinowski (44) writes: "According to a tribal lore the child's body is built exclusively by the mother, the father contributing nothing. There is in every man or woman a spirit. After death it reappears in a woman's body causing pregnancy". Thus transmigration of the soul, a doctrine of Animism, was applied to explain human birth. It is obvious that reproduction was overlooked and this would have required the union of two elements.

Later on when man had taken to pastoral life and saw his animals reproducing, he realized that a male and a female, as partners, jointly contribute to the production of an issue. In Animism even the universe had a soul and it was called Cosmic Soul. Generalizing and abstracting from the phenomenon of reproduction Dualism attributed even to the Cosmic Soul a dual nature. Its male sub-soul was called Yang in Chinese, meaning Light, and the female sub-soul Yin, or Darkness. Man's male sub-soul is called Spirit, and the female counterpart, "the" Soul or Soul-specific. Before Animism had projected the human constitution to everything else. Now Dualism assumed that like the body of man everything was dual-natured being contributions of its own male and female progenitors. Soul was no exception.

26. The two sub-souls.

Soul was constituted of two sub-souls. We are to explain their relative attributes. The male-soul, or Yang-soul is Spirit in English. It is responsible for life-span, the more of it, longer the life. Its synonym would be Growth-soul. It is richest among plants and growth is nowhere so conspicuous as in the vegetable kingdom. The female-soul, or Yin-soul is merely Soul in English, here called *the* Soul or Soul-specific. It confers form, and individuality, properties pertaining to matter or body as the vehicle of Spirit, the life-essence. Metals being hard, heavy and, above all, heat-resistant, are strong-bodied and must harbour a rich proportion of it. As such this sub-soul can be further called Soul-corporeal. Now a herb is delicate and non-resistant to heat. Its Soul-corporeal must be poor. On the contrary a metal which hardly reveals any growth contains Growth-soul as a trace. Then a metal, least capable of growing but most resistant to heat, comes as the opposite of a plant which grows profusely but is easily scorched. They become ideal opposites with their four sub-souls as: Plant=Powerful Growth-soul+Weak Soul-corporeal, Metal=Powerful Soul-corporeal+Weak

Growth-soul. If we now calcine them together a certain temperature would kill the metal, expelling its weak Growth-soul, but leaving the body as a perfect, undecomposed corpse, with its powerful Soul-corporeal within. At the same heat the plant would be left as ashes and its powerful Growth-soul would be hovering to transmigrate into any vehicle. There would be the despirited metal ready to accept any soul. Thus calcining means inducing transmigration of herbal soul into a metallic body but also resurrection of a metal killed by heat but revived by the soul of a plant. Now Spirit, or Growth-soul is common to all vehicles. Paracelsus calls it "the life-force in all created things". Thus when the metal is resurrected by a herbal soul this is not specific. Consequently the calcined metal can be looked upon as the result of reincarnation as also of resurrection. The latter should be resuscitation when its own spirit returns but in Dualism all spirits are Growth-souls and nothing else. The spirit of a plant and of a metal are qualitatively the same.

However according to Animism a calcined metal would represent a clear case of reincarnation. The mono-elemental soul of a plant now transmigrates into a metal which has been forced to part with its own soul. The resultant becomes a metal carrying a herbal soul. Here the calcined metal, herbo-metallic in its make-up, is more of a herb due to its soul, even though it is heavy and powdery like the rust of a metal than like the ashes of a plant. Rust is no metal to the alchemist; rust is dead, metal is living. But herbo-metallic preparation has a soul which donates growth like a plant and makes the body strong like a metal. When the acceptor receives such a substance his body regains robust health and his life-essence grows like a plant which is perennial conferring immortality. However the explanation in the light of Dualism makes "calcined metal" Resurrection Body rather than Reincarnation Body. Nevertheless the real interpretation of calcined metals as Rasayanas being herbo-metallic has to be confirmed.

The Maharaja of Gondal (45) was a regular graduate of medicine, qualified from the Edinburgh University. He therefore can be considered as an authority to explain that the ancient Hindus "have described the method of transferring the properties of vegetable cures to certain metals which intensify their efficacy and retain it a long time." Common sense refuses to accept the transference of herbal properties to a metal. The above statement is an impossible attempt to interpret in terms of rationalism a case clear enough in Animism, of a herbal soul reincarnating in a metal, thereby occupying a vehicle better than the one before.

Briefly, calcined metal is Reincarnation Body according to Animism, but Resurrection Body according to Dualism. A Resurrection Body is a union between two entities clearly as such. The Resurrection Body, two as one, body and soul inseparable from each other, becomes Soul-incorporate. As quoted by J. Read (70; 95) J. E. Mercer explains that, "the alchemists would take a metal, say lead, and calcine it in the air and watch it change into a powdery kind of cinder, red oxide of lead. Assuming, as they did, that a metal had a life (soul) of its own, what was more natural than to say it had died. It was the condition which they imagined a seed would be that had died in the ground. Then they reheated this cinder in a crucible along with some grains of wheat. They watched the metal taking on again its original state. What was more natural than to suppose that the life (soul) in the grain (of wheat) had brought about the resurrection of the metal". Here, there is a donor of soul which is vegetable by nature, and its acceptor is a metal. The calcined lead is clearly a herbo-metallic complex and a Resurrection Body.

27. Pulverization of calcined metals.

If a metal is killed by heat and revived, the vehicle remains corporeal as before. If however it is pulverized, it becomes soul-like and its Soul-corporeal is free to interact with the Growth-soul of the plant and their union becomes perfect. Pulverization kills the metal physically but it is accompanied by herbal extracts so that pulverization with herbal principles means a series of killing and resurrection. According to Philo, the impact of soul upon matter makes it soul-like. The proper effect of juice saturated with soul is to make the corporeal nature of pulverized metal soul-like. Thus the resultant becomes soul-like as also enlivened. Then a Resurrection Body, in turn, is an immortalizing agent. Turning to a materialistic explanation, in a plant, as actually observed, growth stops later on. But a ferment is capable of eternal increase. The herbo-metallic complex is a Resurrection Body as also a ferment. Then alchemy, interpreted as resurrecting a metal, produces Resurrection Body which is an "Immortal Body". And as producing a ferment it takes a dead metal and makes it to grow, not like a plant, but like a ferment as ever-increasing. To resurrect a metal, is to create out of it a living ferment. Remembering Davis maintaining that a "reduced substance is itself a reducer", we can say that an agent made ever-increasing is itself capable of conferring eternal growth. When growth is perfect it explains the other attributes of Archaeus as those which "resist disease, heal and reproduce".

28. Calcined gold as the ideal herbo-metallic preparation.

We have realized that the Reincarnation Body is the achievement of Animism which corresponds to Resurrection Body of Dualism, and both are Immortal Bodies. As such they are also immortalizing agents. Now gold is ever-lasting as body. If it can be enlivened, its corporeal nature, already permanent, would be the easiest to deliver a drug of immortality with its soul ever-growing. Gold otherwise was being taken internally in different ways. To make a herbo-aurous preparation would be to resurrect gold with a herbal soul and produce Gold-ferment better than any metal ferment. Now when gold granules are pulverized with herbal extracts yellow gold turns into a red powder as colloidal gold. The change from yellow to red would be like an anaemic body turning rosy with the colour of ideal health. The original gold was relatively dead, the red gold was pronounced living, in fact resurrected. And herbal extract would be "red-gold-making juice". Since this was living gold or to the alchemist, real gold, he called the juice "gold-making juice". It was really "resurrecting juice". There were herbs that could immortalize man, and the same further, as herbo-metallic or herbo-aurous preparation, could therefore confer immortality via resurrection.

The alchemist, as Animist, conceived everything living; a plant grew best, next a crystal like that of salt, finally a metal. All were living and had the potentialities to grow, just like some seeds germinating later than others. The base metals prone to rust and decay were poor growers and as such could not repair injuries inflicted by the weather. However, when a powerful herb donated its Growth-soul, even a base metal could grow to perfection, which means to a stage when it becomes fire-proof; another way of saying the same is that it becomes gold. Base metals then were like rickety children and their adolescence means gold. But the resultant gold was something forced to grow, and inheriting this power from a plant it becomes Ferment-gold, in turn capable of transmitting power of growth to any acceptor. When a base metal becomes gold there will be no doubt left of its having become a drug of immortality. Taking yellow gold and changing it into red gold is still not so convincing as when say copper becomes gold. That is why the alchemist was after making gold for the agency that brings about such a clear-cut transformation can surely do likewise with an infirm old man. Having once produced gold, it would be Ferment-gold which inoculated into mercury would make the latter grow to be perfect or ever-lasting gold. When this is taken as drug by man, growth will restart repair and renovation and he would acquire robust health; the life-essence ever-increasing would make the drug-made-youth an immortal-youth. By now we realize, how a metal is made to grow with a herbal soul into an eternal and living metal and how the resultant is a ferment first, and gold next, which means Ferment-gold. It is gold to look at but a ferment and an immortalizer by its properties.

The role of a herb in gold-making has now to be confirmed as actually believed. Just as the Maharaja of Gondal explains herbal virtues being transferred on to metals, Mukand Singh (46) depicts a herb mixed with a metal turned the latter into gold. He met a bogus master of alchemy. The latter ordered a copper coin being produced. Then the master gave Mukand Singh a fresh herb to be mixed with tobacco; the mixture was filled in a clay smoking-pipe into which was also placed the coin. When smoking reached its end and the contents of the pipe were tipped over, the copper had changed into gold. It was the herb that was the gold-making agent when its juice would be gold-making juice. This term translated into Chinese means Kim-Iya, literally Gold-juice, but best interpreted as gold-making juice. The herb is the vehicle of its juice, and juice a concentrate of Growth-soul. There are many versions of the belief that some rare plants can make gold. The implied property of growth-acceleration is properly transmitted by such legends. Thus by now we can say that Charaka's Rasayana, or the art of rejuvenation-cum-immortality when extended to metals, becomes alchemy, which treats them as rickety children growing into adolescence-cum-immortality. In both, Rasayana and alchemy, the agent is herbal, in both the aim is immortality. Rasayana treats an infirm old patient, while alchemy a rickety metal first and through it the same old patient. Thus the chief objectives of the two were to acquire the power of transmuting base metals into gold and to prepare an elixir which could impart immortality to human beings. Herb at once becomes important as the donor of Growth-soul and the elixir left unspecified becomes clear when it is identified with synthetic gold or Ferment-gold.

29. Other systems of gaining longevity.

We have shown that Rasayana, though really geriatrics, lies on the border land of alchemy which attempts to rejuvenate man and treat base metals as rickety systems. Had there been enthusiasts attempting to synthesize gold among his contemporaries Charaka would have certainly mentioned it. In China there also existed two other cults of longevity. One was concerned with deep breathing exercises and its counterpart in India is found as a branch of Yoga system. Charaka (on p. 497) refers to "open air modes of vitalization". He lived up north and what he refers to would be sun-bath or light-therapy analogous to what is popular in Northern Europe.

The other Chinese cult can be described as "Gymnastics in sexual intercourse". Prof. Needham (47) in his classic on Chinese Civilization has referred to it and the same appears to have been introduced into India by founders of the Tantric cult who are also the pioneers of Indian (mercurial) alchemy. Some Indian temple sculpture depicts scenes of such sexual gymnastics. Obviously they do not reveal increasing sexual pleasure but have to be interpreted as exploiting ejaculated semen to be absorbed within the body thereby strengthening it and increasing life. A modern physician in Bangladesh looks upon intramuscular injection of one's own blood as a panacea. Correspondingly auto-assimilation of one's own semen is another. Later, mercurials were compared with semen and thereby considered as life-prolonging drugs; in fact mercury has been called "Shiva's semen"; and Shiva was once an old sage who later became young, almost a Cupid. However what particularly interests us here is that we find no trace of it in Charaka (24). On p. 501 he speaks of "Woman the best virilific". But this refers to normal sex life of a young man. On the contrary on p. 513 he definitely opines that, "sex-act is contra-indicated for an old man". Thus it seems that the Tantric system of "sexual gymnastics" was imported later from China, like alchemy. What has to be seen further is that union of opposites here is actually between a pair of opposite sexes and as generating "creative force" to be assimilated by the male member. The theory that union of opposites leads to creative power appears here in its most undisguised form. Later on, in paragraph 46, the opposites become Shiva/Parvati or Hara/Gauri, and their union projected to that between Mercury/Mica, these being personified at the same time. Only when we realize the existence of such Tantric cults, called here "sexual gymnastics", that we thoroughly understand the origin and development of Dualism and its exploitation in alchemy. The two run on parallel lines.

30. The beginning of alchemy.

In China there must have existed herbalism promising immortality just as it did in India. It must be looked upon as herbal magic promising something impossible to contrast with herbalism proper as the system of treating ailments with plants. Chinese pictures depict legendary immortals carrying a leaf representing a plant, as also a mushroom not to talk of distillates of such plants preserved sealed in gourds. Such a picture has been reproduced in an earlier article by me (40). Apart from plants, the Chinese also tried red minerals. This requires reverting to a past which recommends such a selection.

We have discussed that the earliest concept of Soul equates it, not with breath or air in movement, but with blood. Blood = Soul, then Redness = Soul. Cavemen of Central Europe as also of China all used to smear the remains of the dead with red ochre. The custom still survives, for Birket-Smith (48; 218) found it existing among the Moris of New Zealand. They "clear the bones of the dead, colour red and then bury in a distant cave". The Chinese later used minium or red oxide of lead, and finally cinnabar, red sulphide of mercury. Purifying by fire the ores of minium they got lead, which became its essence, and lead finds such a place in the earliest theory of Chinese alchemy, which recognizes lead from which all metals are made. Unable to distinguish cinnabar from minium and refining them together they later got also mercury, at once striking by its heaviness and shining appearance. Sulphur must have escaped observation for it is very volatile and in the earlier days the technique was imperfect. Thus from a red ore, but of a mixed nature, they got lead and mercury, which became the two elements from which even gold was made. This phase of alchemy is usually overlooked. With better familiarity with red ores the Chinese found nothing so close to red blood as cinnabar. This became the drug of immortality. No other people interned cinnabar with the dead nor took it orally as a drug. Waley (49) informs that, "with human remains and on the objects associated with them as Hsin-Cheng bronzes of 6th Cent. B.C. the nature of red pigment according to Pelliot is cinnabar" (p. 18). Waley himself remarks: "Where outside China, do we first meet with the idea of eating the product of alchemical fusion (or synthetic cinnabar called vermilion) of using not merely as healer of metals but also as a medicine for man (p. 21)". To be able to make cinnabar so important, familiarity with it must have a long past. And Waley (p. 19) does explain that "an alchemy concerned merely with the fabrication of cinnabar no doubt goes back to very early times. When the cinnabar has been made, the gold will follow without further difficulty". This naturally implies that the Chinese fully recognized cinnabar as soul of minerals and metals and sulphur and mercury as sub-souls which in right proportion produced gold. The "Sulphur-Mercury" theory came to stay for ever. But what has not to be overlooked is that synthetic gold was to be the ideal drug of immortality. Here there were opposite sub-souls and union between them ideal as gold. Let us here consider the juice Soma. It was rich in one sub-soul and could serve as a drug-of-immortality but had to be taken regularly. All herbal drugs were largely mono-elemental like Soma. A herbo-metallic complex on the other hand was constituted of two opposites, or two sub-souls in union. But these sub-souls came from different sources. On the contrary mercury and sulphur had a common origin as parts of cinnabar so that they, as sub-souls, could fuse better than the essence of a herb with a metal. It amounts to saying that to start with mercury and sulphur as sub-souls is as good as merely reconditioning cinnabar the soul. Thus Waley himself looks upon alchemical gold as "super-cinnabar". This is why he writes that "when cinnabar has been made, gold will follow without further difficulty". The difficulty is removed by the theory that the sub-souls of cinnabar are the two elements of gold as of any other metal but the difficulty would persist in experimentally carrying out that theory. However we can construct the series Blood=Soul=Redness=Cinnabar=Sulphur+Mercury. We can now realize how cinnabar and mercurials became special preparations of pharmaceutical chemistry in the past and this was real alchemy.

31. Herbalism in China as progenitor of alchemy.

Herbal magic was spread all over the world and

persists in disguised forms even today. Just as Indians calcined metals with plants, the Chinese must have also calcined minerals with herbs to more than purify them. In their term Kim-Iya, Iya is primarily a juice, which is capable of making gold, Kim. We have seen how a gold-making herb was used while rehearsing an experiment in gold synthesis. Purifying minerals with herbal juices must have also been popular in China. At any rate we have first to respect the primary sense of Iya, as fresh plant juice, and only then Kim-Iya can signify gold-making juice in preference to any other connotation attributable to it. Probably along with the use of cinnabar herbs were also used, the two went to produce an enhanced effect. Later a herb and mineral gave a purified mineral or virtually a herbo-mineral preparation. My knowledge here does not permit showing how an experiment, similar to what Mukand Singh describes, must have been accepted as typical also in China. Their alchemy advanced much further transcending herbalism as did also that of the Arabs both of which became mainly mineral or chemical. Then mercurials as drugs of immortality were introduced from China into India and alchemy came at the same time.

32. Kashmir as connecting India with China.

Buddhism spread to China from where Swat lies in Pakistan. Contacts between India and China included Kashmir as the most popular connecting link between the two continents. Stein (50; vol. II, p. 354) informs that, "the first reference to Kashmir is a record from 541 A.D. during the early T'ang dynasty, ninety years later being the visit of Hsiung Tsiang". "The first embassy from Kashmir by its Kings Chandrapida and Muktapida, was about 713 A. D." (p. 357). "In Kashmir of 8th Cent. there was a foreigner as minister, Cankuna from Tukhara land, north of Kashmir". Prof. Sylvan Levi "equates Chankuna=Tsiang-Kiun but considers the Sanskrit name a transcription of the

Chinese title" (vol. I, p. 143). "Chankuna founded the Cankuna Vihara...This minister from Tukhara land occupied an important position at Lalitaditya's Court (in 8th Cent.)". Now in vol. I, p. 147 we read that, "producing plenty of gold in the treasury by magic power he gave him (the king) comfort". The latter statement belongs to some legend. But production of gold as a legend can nevertheless be traced to a previous notion that gold can be synthesized. Not more need be discussed what is not historical. We are however certain that by the 6th Cent. Kashmir had received alchemy from China to have legends, as above, current in 8th Cent. The predominant religion at the time in Kashmir was Shivaism, which in turn harboured Tantric cults. Here I have no further information of value since the origin of Tantrics itself remains uninvestigated. It nevertheless seems probable that alchemy was practised in India during 6th Cent. It was unknown in 3rd Cent.

33. Indian alchemy probably begins about 500 A.D.

Prof. Winternitz (51) critically reviews the position of India with respect to the use of mercury. He writes (on p. 100) that, "It is of great importance that Kautilya (the author of a work on the principles of state administration) among different kinds of gold mentions artificial gold (which is also mentioned in the History of Kashmir) made from other metals by chemical process in which mercury is used. Now the use of mercury both in alchemy and in medicine is well known in India, but is found only in later literature. Even P. C. Ray in his excellent History of Indian Chemistry (he believes that alchemy is indigenous to India) cannot trace it back any further than the earliest Tantric text in the 5th or 6th Cent. A. D. In medicinal works mercury is mentioned only once in Charaka's treatise, once in the Bower M.S. of 4th Cent. A. D. and twice in Susrutha. It is entirely unknown in earlier literature...This chapter on minerals (must be) of later origin to the Arthasastra (as originally composed by Kautilya)".

Confirming Winternitz, Prof. Stappleton (52) writes as follows: "Mercury was known and used in Europe, Near East and China, for hundreds of years, before the first mention of it appears in Indian medicinal works. In China, Tan-Sha, Mercuric Sulphide (cinnabar), was the Elixir of life from at least 200 B. C. It is all the more necessary to emphasize this, as very recently Sir P. C Ray, in strange disregard to the mass of published work on the subject, including the striking evidence of the actual texts, of his own in the History of Hindu Chemistry, has again stated that the knowledge of pharmacy which the Arabs brought to Europe, specially the use of Mercury, should be credited to India".

However from a short article in *Isis* we learn from Filliozat (53; 363) of the "existence of alchemy long before the time supposed by P. C. Ray". If calcined metals were alchemical preparations then Indian alchemy is old. But if alchemy is to be restricted as preparing mercurials then it is a later introduction from China. Legends cannot be valued unless we know the existence or absence first of a cult that seriously took to synthesizing gold, using mercury, not magic as mentioned in the History of Kashmir. Moreover synthetic gold was drug of immortality, whereas magical gold a substitute of metallic gold. However if we grant that India imported alchemy from China its development in India as relatively fast can be easily appreciated.

34. Alchemy in India about 1000 A. D.

Alchemy is the art of rejuvenation using mercurials. Rasayana is the generic term for the art of rejuvenation which first started with the use of herbal mixtures and ended by preferring mercurials. We have seen that

Charaka mentions drugs of rejuvenation, recognizing the art as a physician. About 800 A. D. lived another master of Indian medicine comparable with Galen in Greek medicine. He is known as Vagbhatta. Whereas Charaka had two divisions, Vagbhatta has eight. Medicine comprising of eight departments was called Ashtanga, "constituted of eight members". Monier-Williams (31; 118) translates the term Ashtanga as "of eight parts" and enumerates all of them. The two that interest us are "Rasayana-Tantra or the doctrine of Elixirs and Vajikarana-Tantra or the doctrine of aphrodisiacs". The latter may be useful to some youths but the doctrine of rejuvenation is clearly geriatrics, conceived by the earliest ascetics of India, confirmed by Charaka, and finally recognized by Vagbhatta, the Galen of India. We should not be surprised then if Alberuni speaks of it as a well-recognized system in India, and overlooks alchemy and mercurials as medicine or even gold-making. We are not interested here in alchemy as such or in its doctrines, but in its history. And we merely notice that Alberuni speaks of Nagarjuna, by name, who lived about 800 A. D. and occupies a position in Indian mercurial alchemy comparable to that of Jabir Ibn Hayyan in that of Islamic. When Sir P.C. Ray refers to the position of Indian alchemy about 1000 A. D. his main authority has been Alberuni (9). He was an acute observer differentiating the views of the intelligentsia from the beliefs of the crowd. He has therefore realized the special feature of Indian medicine, the like of which he missed in Muslim countries. Alberuni lived in India from 1017-1030 A.D., and found at the time that, the Hindus "have a science similar to alchemy which is peculiar to them. They call it Rasayana, a word composed with Rasa, i.e. gold. It means the art which is restricted to certain operations, drugs and compound medicines, most of which are taken from plants. Its principles restore health of those who were ill beyond hope and gave back youth to fading old age so that people become again what they were in the age near puberty (and) restored the capacity of juvenile agility (with robust health) and even (that) for cohabitation". Charaka also spoke of rejuvenated sages becoming "attractive to women". Moreover Alberuni dispenses in these few words that, "calcination and sublimation inclined towards mineralogical method of alchemy."Yet this is not alchemy proper for Charaka does mention calcined metals or herbo-metallic preparations. Mere mention of Nagarjuna by name and cursorily referring to "mineralogical alchemy" merely shows that Rasayanas, as existing then, were same as in Charaka's age, and what were not yet popular about 1000 A. D. were mercurial drugs and alchemy as the art of gold-making.

35. Momiyai a panacea of later origin in India.

Alberuni (9) also refers to legends specifying them as such. On (p. 190) he records that, "a book on Rasayana according to a legend contains the prescription of a medicine made with Oil and Human Blood both being required". In this connection he mentions the preparation Raktamala. Now such a medicament does exist and its latest designation is Momiyai. Raktamala is mentioned by Alberuni as existing in a legendary work. Sachau (on p. 315) explains its etymology as Rakta=Red, and Amala=*Phyllanthus emblica* or Red-Amala. But Alberuni clearly mentions its constituents as "Oil and Human Blood" so that Rakta=Blood and with Amala, Raktamala may be "Blood and Amala". I am unable to further interpret Raktamala etymologically, but I am certain that it is a preparation with human blood so that Raktamala=Momiyai. Momiyai in turn is best conceived as the substitute of mummy as drug. Possibly the name Momiyai itself is also traceable to mummy. Foote (54) illustrates an actual Egyptian mummy and further states that it was a "famous cure-all of the dark ages...The medieval medicine-man imported it in its original mummy case from the banks of the Nile (as) a sure panacea for all the ills that flesh is heir to...Dried mummy was a favourite remedy... There was much substitution and bodies were dried in imitation of the genuine article...(there was a) formula consisting of a distillate of human bones." Thus human remains were also exploited as medicaments. And Momiyai obviously belongd to this category.

Momiyai is described by Mookerji (55) who was a professional physician of the Indian system of medicine or Ayurveda. In a Sanskrit text quoted (p. 57) it is termed "Human Oil". The author's commentary (on p. 293) explains it as follows: "It is human fat that can be obtained in a most cruel manner. A human hermaphrodite is to be fed with nutritious food to make the creature sufficiently fat. It is then to be flayed alive and hanged with his feet upwards and head downwards, kept suspended over an iron cauldron, heated by a strong fire. When sufficiently heated, fat begins to come out of the body of the unfortunate creature and falls into the cauldron. This fat is very efficacious in instantly healing wounds and cuts in animal bodies. This is the oil which according to tradition, the physician Asvini Kumara applied to joining the goat's head to the body of King Daksha who had been beheaded by his son-in-law and thereby effected a resurrection of the dead". Tucker (56; note 459) explains "Brain Oil, Momiyai—Capture a child hang it up by the heels over a cauldron of boiling oil, puncture the skull, the brain oil will then exude. This brain oil fetches high prices as a styptic for fresh wounds. It is now very difficult to procure." G. Woulfe (56; note 1073) confirms writing, "Mamia; catch a lad, the blacker the better, fatten him on fruits without salt and bread. When he is fat hang him by the heels to a tripod over a cauldron of boiling Ghee (butter), tap the centre of the skull, letting the blood fall into the cauldron. Internally it is an aphrodisiac and cures impotence...All Hakims (Muslim physicians) and Baids (Hindu Ayurvedic physicians) make thus". Here we have the right indications: Momiyai is blood-in-oil preparation. It heals wounds when externally used, but cures impotency thereby amounting to rejuvenation, when used internally. Perhaps the most candid confirmation of its existence is the observation by Millet (56; note 852) in reply to the remark of Tucker stating that, "there are still European officials in Simla who make brain oil from natives. Their Chaprasis (messengers) kidnap children and others for the purpose". What I do wish to emphasize is the incorporation of human blood in Momiyai, correctly recorded by Alberuni, though the source was legendary but it is confirmed by Woulfe. That human blood could also be incorporated in a calcined metal is clearly mentioned by Mookerji (55; 57). He writes that, "Mica (the Indian substitute of lead when Lead-Mercury were the two elements of all metals) is to be powdered very fine and subjected to calcination with Human Oil (Momiyai)". Here calcined mica would be human blood-in-mica, like herbal juice-in-metal. Blood is soul and on calcining, blood as soul, reincarnates itself in mica. For such a preparation first Momiyai is made and then calcined with mica.

To understand Momiyai we must appreciate mummy as drug. Mummy is a body, immune to decomposition unlike any corpse. It is ever-lasting like gold in the form of dried body. Then both, mummy and gold, are corporeal vehicles of soul, each in itself ever-lasting. Blood is soul and in the mummy the entire blood has been preserved, so that any piece of mummy, though dried flesh, actually signifies dried blood or incorporated soul. Had blood been expelled and only the flesh dried, there would have been no soul. When Momiyai is prepared, blood, the soul, is well conserved in oil. It is otherwise naturally preserved in the mummy. Thus mummy is superior to flesh without blood, as also to blood which has not been conserved properly. In preparing Momiyai it is precisely human blood, and not human flesh, that becomes its main ingredient and attributes assigned to Momiyai are precisely those of blood or of soul. As in a herbo-metallic preparation metal is the vehicle, in Momiyai, oil is the vehicle and blood as good as soul. Not fat but blood is the content, then blood at its best, coming from the brain, the seat of intelligence. Woulfe has correctly interpreted Momiyai as a blood preparation. The one virtue attributed to Momiyai is the power to heal wounds, a phenomenon which in turn best reveals the power of growth of indolent or inert tissue. And taken internally, Momiyai would diffuse into the system and make every organ and gland grow to its full capacity and thus drive away disease, be it anywhere. This qualifies it as a panacea.

36. Drug-induced sublimation of the material body.

The same legend in Alberuni maintains that the "Oil and Human Blood" preparation, when "besmeared (makes the individual) fly up in the air". The change is the same which occurred with the body of Jesus after resurrection as ascension. It is the property of Resurrection Body. The all-changing agent here is Blood as soul. Claverley (57) points out that, "Al-Shaharastani in his description of the belief of pagan Arabs does not use the terms Ruh (Spirit) and Nafs (Soul-specific) but says that blood becomes Wraith-bird", which would be an incarnation. And Birket-Smith (48; 17) would add that, "among aborigines there is a strong belief that blood possesses magical powers". Thus what we call soul was blood to the primitive man who however attributed to it magical, really creative powers, such as soul alone can possess. One such power was to transform itself into a bird, when Bird = Soul-incorporate. This conception was entertained not only by Arabs but, as Nilsson (58; 102) informs, that even in Greece the idea of "soul bird was extremely common". It could also be confirmed by Indonesian art-symbolism. Thus the blood-in-oil preparation, on being smeared on the body, made the latter soul-like, expressed by its power of moving about as though space did not exist and also to fly up in the air. It can easily make the same individual invisible at will. Jildaki (59), a famous Muslim alchemist, also gives such particulars qualifying a man who has taken Elixir. We have seen that a powerful drug is effective even on physical contact, and herbal magic, in particular, is based on such a hypothesis. The same taken internally would naturally prove more effective. The "blood-in-oil" preparation of the legend is externally applied, yet it can sublimate the material body making it soul-like; and it is also a panacea, both the properties being mentioned in Alberuni. There is a Chinese legend according to which a prince of Hui Nan took some Elixir and what was left was licked up by his dog and the rest picked by a cock. All died but all revived and they ascended to Heaven in broad day light just as Jesus did. The scene has been illustrated and I have reproduced the picture in an earlier article (41). Such a drug-made-immortal in Chinese is called Hsien-Shen. Davis (60) concluded that such a being is identical with the Jinn of "Arabian Nights" and the word "Jinn" must necessarily be Chinese. I (61) have been able to confirm this etymology.

37. Legends of gold with the power of growth.

There is a second legend reproduced by Alberuni (9) referring to a "Rasayana which would make one immortal" (p. 191). Thus it is clear that Rasayana rejuvenates and it also immortalizes. But it does even more, it makes one "victorious and capable of doing everything one desires" (p. 191). If I may so put it, it is like Aladin's lamp as a drug, or a drug with similar powers to those of Aladin's lamp. Even this notion is Chinese. A third story (p. 192) refers to a "plant of the species of Lactaria from which blood flows, otherwise a milky sap oozes out". Such a plant was exploited by tricking a man who was thrown into fire and was burnt with the herb. The man was accompanied by a dog and the bodies of both became golden. We have to focus attention on the active principle turning even flesh, be it of man or of dog, into gold. It was apparently a herb but the juice of the herb was blood-like or as good as blood. Once we get to blood, it is soul which is a miraculous, all-transforming agent. The legend makes a plant the vehicle of soul or at least of Redness, and plant is an entity that grows. Thus the Redness of plant imparts the resultant gold the power of growth. And the legend is quite explicit on this point. A peasant seeing the body of gold "cut off a finger" and bought food-stuffs with it. But next day when "he returned to the golden man where the cut finger had been, a new finger had grown."

I tried to pursue if such an interesting story has survived. Mrs. Postans (62) found, in 1839, that "all the people of Cutch believe in the Waters of life and in Philosopher's Stone". She narrates a legend attributed to the reign of a king named Lakhi, when a man was burnt as above, by a stratagem, using a special herb with red juice, with which the body, so to say, was calcined. The result produced a golden body of the man. But this could grow, for any member cut away will be replaced by a fresh one. The herb changed flesh into gold but gold was something living capable of self-repair or growth. The most important point here is the red juice of the herb recalling Redness = Soul.

Subsequent to the compilation of this monograph, Dr. Baloch (108) Vice-Chancellor of Sind University, kindly presented me with a copy of History of Thatta town written in 1621 which he has edited.

In the accompanying letter he rightly points out that the legend which begins on p. 67 is entitled Tora-Purs but instead it should be Tila-Purs since the author himself translates the term in Persian as Golden-Man. Tila=Gold and Purusha=Man, in Sanskrit. Accordingly, Tila-Purusha would be the correct Persian-Sanskrit term enabling us to state that Chin-Jen (Chinese)=Tora-Purs=Tila-Purusha=Golden-Man, each being literally translated. Their proper significance makes them Gold-made-immortal, a man who has acquired immortality by using alchemical gold as drug. Literally taken the term Golden-Man degenerates into a Figure-of-gold on which the legend is based. It begins by reference to Cutch where a goat was observed with its mouth red. An ascetic there was aware that a herb with its blood-red juice has the property of transforming a substance into gold when calcined with it. Obviously the goat had eaten such a herb which actually proved to be its sole food-plant. There further appeared a shepherd whom he induced to cooperate in setting up a fire with the object of worshipping it and the fire was lit up with that herb. As the ritual, the ascetic and the shepherd were to go round and round the fire. The ascetic had planned thereby to throw the shepherd into the fire, and calcine him into gold. The shepherd sensed the danger and instead managed to throw the ascetic into the fire when he turned into a figure of gold. He cut out an arm but next day found the same had grown to replace what was missing. Thus the legend confirms the belief in a gold-making herb, the carrier of a gold-making juice (Kimiya) and the plant incorporated Redness as the active principle, best appreciated as Soul, and that synthetic gold incorporates the power of growth donated by the plant which thus makes alchemical gold a living substance.

Such a legend has given the latest version I could trace as reported in 1948. In a preface to a book on cookery Aga Hyder Hassan (63), Professor of Urdu,

Nizam's College, Hyderabad, India, relates as follows: "It has been narrated that the chief of the Royal kitchen of King Vajid Ali Shah, of Lucknow, would prepare a dish of lentils *(dal)* by first frying a gold coin in Ghee (butter). To verify such a strange recipe the King had the procedure demonstrated. After frying, the gold coin was thrown away and the Ghee, with which the coin was fried, was poured on a dry tree trunk or block of wood. When the coin was examined, the hard metallic gold had become a crumbling mass on being pressed between fingers and on the next day the dry stump began to sprout." As far as the tree trunk was concerned it was resurrected or made to grow like a living tree. The causal factor, with the power of growth, was obviously in the gold where it lay in a potential or latent form. By heating it was transferred and now Ghee became the vehicle of that power in its dynamic phase. When this Ghee was poured on a dried trunk as dead plant it was revived and could grow. Though the tree was resurrected the phenomenon can also be interpreted as a case of reincarnation. The Growth-soul infused in gold left the coin as dead and went over into the tree trunk. Caricatures exaggerate intrinsic but subtle characters. Legends do the same, making them attractive and impressive. That alchemical gold is Ferment-gold and not the same as metallic gold or fossil gold no history of alchemy brings out into prominence. On the other hand the legends narrated above clearly attribute to gold the power of growth, when gold becomes something living. That is why legends were not ignored in this study.

38. Etymology of Rasayana.

The best evidence is internal evidence or what the word itself connotes; in this case it is Rasayana. According to Sir P.C. Ray, Rasa=Mercury and Ayana=Way, when Rasayana=Way to Mercury, the know-how of mercury. Such an etymology was coined to identify

Rasayana as alchemy proper or mercurial alchemy. But we have seen Charaka uses the term Rasayana earlier for the art of rejuvenation and for drugs employed by that art. With Charaka, Rasayana was mainly herbal and only next partly so. He does not speak of any mercurial. Then Alberuni makes the root, Rasa=Gold. Rasa has several meanings. Its original meaning is Rasa=Juice, freshly extracted from a plant. It is identical with the word Iya of Chinese, in the term Kim-Iya (Arabic Kimiya). Now the Sanskrit Bengali Dictionary, Amartha-Chandrika (64), translates Rasa=Pran. Since Pran=Life-essence or Soul, Rasa=Soul. We have had the formula Blood=Soul. Then what is blood to man is juice to a plant so that Blood=Juice=Soul. In a legend reported just before, a plant contained blood as its juice or juice was blood. This notion enables interpreting, Blood=Rasa=Soul, the juice as soul of plant. In Dualism all Growth-souls are qualitatively identical, though not quantitatively, and Blood as also Juice are growth producers.

So far no one has paid any attention to Alberuni's etymology, Rasa=Gold, so vital in alchemy as the art of gold-making. Obviously his information was derived from some Sanskrit Pandit whom he consulted. To vindicate his etymology there is Gossain's (65) Bengali to Bengali Dictionary where Rasa=Swarna and Swarna=Gold. Thus Rasa=Gold. By now we have the renderings: Rasa=Juice=Soul=Gold. The equation Rasa=Gold can be confirmed by justifying Gold=Soul. Gold is the only substance on earth which is fire-proof, thus ever-lasting. According to our conception, soul is eternal. Thus at least in the sense that gold and soul are both ever-lasting, Gold=Soul. According to Dualism, a metal has a large ratio of Soul-corporeal but a negligible one of Growth-soul. But in gold, the Soul-corporeal is at its maximum which makes it fire-proof. Then referring to Soul-corporeal, in particular, gold is practically nothing else than Soul-corporeal. In this light Gold has been taken to prolong life.

We now turn to the suffix Ayana of Rasayana. The best rendering is found in the popular Bengali to Bengali Dictionary of Mitra (66). Here Ayana=Ashra and Ashra=Shelter, hence also Abode and Vehicle. Then one rendering makes Rasayana=Vehicle of Juice, when Juice=Soul. Now the translation of Rasayana, as Vehicle of juice, compares ideally with Gildemeister's (67; p. 537) rendering of the later Greek word for alchemy which is Chumeia. According to him Chumeia "is a concrete noun in the sense of *medium containing juice*". Here the Greek root is Chumos= Juice, like Rasa. The suffix is Eia=pertaining to, comparable with—Ayana=Vehicle. Thus as actually etymologized by Gildemeister, Chumeia=Rasayana. The real significance of Rasayana and of Chumeia would identify each as the fountain-head of soul, of creative energy. Each is a concrete noun and juice-incorporate. In fact I look upon Chumeia as a translation of the Sanskrit word Rasayana. The effective paraphrase however of Rasayana would be Soul-incorporate with Rasa=Soul. Soul being a most active content its container is ignorable when Rasayana is soul in its dynamic form as ever-growing. When Rasa=Gold= Soul then Rasayana=Vehicle of gold, as soul. Here we can compare it with Devayana=Vehicle of gods, a celestial carriage. Rasayana, as Vehicle of gold, would be a synonym of herbo-aurous preparation. Gold would be the vehicle and herb used in its preparation as soul. The end result is identical with, soul-and-its vehicle, the two as one, or Soul-incorporate, appearing as live-gold. The usual commercial term would be "calcined gold", the best among calcined metals or herbo-metallic preparations. It is in such a sense that Alberuni used the word Rasayana with Rasa=Gold. In all the terms composed with the root Rasa, this invariably signifies Soul, as something eternal and something capable of growth, for this is the essential feature of life. Then Rasayanas become donors of growth and thereby of life. Here the original sense of Rasa as juice has undergone transformation for juice of a herb makes it grow and every other Rasa is a substitute of plant juice as soul, the ideal growth principle.

Since the word Rasa, as incorporated in the term Rasayana, has different meanings but all capable of being interpreted as promoting growth or increase, they are briefly listed below:

1. Rasa=Juice, in all Dictionaries
2. Rasa=Jal=Life (Abdul Hamid; 72)
3. Rasa=Prana=Life (Amartha-Chandrika; 64)
4. Rasa=Retha=Semen Virile (Gossain; 65)
5. Rasa=Jal=Water (Gossain; 65)
6. Rasa=Gold (Alberuni; 9 and Gossain; 65)

39. Rasayana as Elixir.

Goethe has made a pregnant observation to the effect that no man knows his own language best unless he knows at least another. The same principle is clear enough when we try to exchange our own currency with another. Let us then see how Rasayana, as used by Charaka, can be rendered into English. The one dictionary we can consult here is that of Monier-Williams (31). It paraphrases Rasayana as "a medicine supposed to prevent old age and prolong life." And when it uses one word for it the translation becomes Rasayana = Elixir. Now Elixir is an Arabicized Chinese term there being no word of Greek or Latin origin which conveys the same sense. And this is because neither Hippocrates, who belonged to Greece, nor Galen, who lived in Rome, recognized rejuvenation as possible. Charaka and Indian physicians, even of modern times, theoretically admit it as a probability. The Chinese, whose medicine was also founded by ascetics, likewise recognized rejuvenation as possible and this takes us to the etymology of Elixir. The word

Elixir has been discussed before (41). The Chinese term is Ik-Ch'i, Ch'i=Soul and Ik-Ch'i=the "one soul", above all others. If ordinary souls account for longevity of different durations "the one soul" is powerful enough to make its acceptor ever-lasting. Ch'i as soul requires merely explaining what soul itself stands for. Soul is a familiar word and we do not fully appreciate on that account its real significance. Rationalists attempting to explain Ch'i have unwittingly described what they themselves conceived soul to be. It is best to allow the Chinese themselves to explain soul. We learn from Edkins (68; 110) that, "a Taoist priest denied that creation was God's act, and maintained that it was the act of material agent which he called Ch'i (character 1064 in Giles) a word meaning a very pure form of matter (=Prime Matter of the alchemist) and was the Creator of things. Its purer part arose and formed Heaven and its grosser portion became Earth". And Giles explains Ch'i as "a vivifying principle" which really means all-creative and all-changing power. Ch'i then has the same powers as Heaven and Earth. Nothing can contrast the significance attributed to Elixir as explained above than equating it, as Sarton (109) has done, Elixir=Tonic. By tonic is meant a medicament strengthening the system as a whole, whereas Elixir would be vivifying the system as a whole, changing a mortal into an immortal. The term used by early Greek alchemists has been "Medicine of Life" mentioned by Taylor (1; 59). It can be improved upon as ' Medicine of Immortal Life" or the drug of immortality.

The alchemist recognized an entity called "Prime Matter", matter itself as primordial element and source of all forms of matter. It was the ever-lasting and self-changing substance. By assigning it such virtues, Prime Matter becomes Soul-incorporate and thus Prime Matter a synonym of "the one soul" or Elixir. This is common to all growing and living forms and can be extracted practically from all substances, if only proper technique is applied. It merely means that instead of placing energy as the original creative power we have Prime Matter instead. One may say that Elixir permeating a base metal transformed it into something living, and since the substance was a metal it became a living metal, and further ever-lasting, which means the resultant became Ferment-gold, ever-lasting and eternally growing. The other version would maintain that a base metal was reduced to Prime Matter which can retransform itself into an ever-lasting, ever-growing form or Ferment-gold. Thus Prime Matter=Elixir. With Ch'i=Soul (in Elixir) and Rasa=Soul (in Rasayana) finally Ch'i equates Elixir, and Rasa equates Rasayana. With Elixir as "the One-soul" incorporate and Rasayana as "Soul-incorporate" we can appreciate Rasayana = Elixir. Even Rasa = Elixir, as given in Monier-Williams (31).

40. Kimiya=Elixir.

We can further proceed to cofirm what has just been stated We know already that in Arabic Iksir = Kimiya so that if Iksir is "the One-soul incorporate"; what does Kimiya signify. This has also been explained before (69). Kim = gold and Iya = juice when Kimiya = gold-making juice. Enough has been said to the effect that the ascetic was not concerned with making gold but instead with making himself young and thereby automatically immortal. The agency he conceived as leading to rejuvenation was a drug which itself can be imagined as having been juvenated, and transformed if not also resurrected. Base metals were under-developed rickety systems. If they could be made to grow continuously to their maximum capacity and remain ever-lasting as well, they would be transformed first into gold, for it is ever-lasting, and also into a ferment, for ferment is ever-growing. They then became the donors of the same virtues to a decrepit old man. The drug then becomes Ferment-gold;

nothing less can be so convincing as a drug of immortality. That is why the alchemist wanted to make gold and only live-gold or Ferment-gold. When this was heated or melted the ferment was killed and dead - gold became the bullion gold we all know. Then generation or reproduction as a property of life was conceived as simply bringing opposites into proper juxtaposition; it was like bringing together a couple, young and beautiful, when they are bound to face as bride and bridegroom. Jildaki thus depicts bringing the two opposite elements as the fundamental step in synthesizing gold. As mentioned by Read (70; 304) Mercury and Sulphur are "our Solar and Lunar Seeds (which make them grow and increase)", thus generating a life-form capable of Growth and Reproduction, exemplified by a ferment. The sulpho-mercurial complex then becomes two-as-one an autonomous self-generating entity. Returning to the term Kim-Iya, as gold-making juice, with juice = soul already explained, Kimiya means gold-making soul. When this is applied to a metal, as was rehearsed by an alchemist before Mukand Singh, the resultant gold incorporated the juice of a growing plant as soul. Even the legend of gold coin assumes delivering its active principle as the power of growth to Ghee and this forcing a dead tree trunk to grow, when gold is the vehicle of Growth-soul. Then the gold-making soul changed a base metal into gold by entering into the latter with the resultant as soul-in-gold or gold now as the carrier of Growth-soul. Briefly, it was Soul-incorporate, with the form of gold. As Soul-incorporate, Kimiya becomes a synonym of Elixir, as also of Rasayana, each having been explained before. In Rasayana, Rasa is juice as soul, in Kimiya, Iya again is juice as soul, in Elixir Ch'i is clearly soul.

41. Drugs of rejuvenation, Chinese and Indian, as reaching Alexandria.

There are legends assuming natural substances as

rejuvenating and immortalizing man. The earliest seems to be water, as in a Fountain of Youth. Next Water of Life as Elixir of Youth and Immortality. Then there were herbs growing in deep waters apparently as having imbibed the powers of water. Finally there was Soma and even vegetable preparations like Amarita and Ambrosia. In historical times we have had Rasayana and Momiyai and finally, as existing even today, Makara Dhwaja. Then water, as causing vegetative growth, and plants as growing entities, incorporate the causal or active principle as growth-inducing power. Of most powers in nature, growth is very impressive so much so that Growth = Life. The abstract notion of Life identifies it with Soul when this becomes an all-becoming and all-changing power, with growth as the most conspicuous property. On attributing all-changing powers to a plant, itself as carrier of soul, there arose herbal magic. On the same principle also arose mineral magic. This has been briefly explained as follows. Starting with Redness as Soul, the Chinese at first had a mixed ore of minium and cinnabar. Purifying it by fire they got lead and mercury. Briefly, a Red mineral = Soul = Lead + Mercury, the latter being sub-souls. When this theory reached India it was modified giving as sub-souls mica and mercury. No one has tried to interpret their origin which can only be understood as modifications of the early Chinese theory with lead and mercury as the two elements which make all other metals and minerals. Later the Chinese could properly select cinnabar as the best substitute of blood in colour. This made Cinnabar = Soul and its two components Sulphur and Mercury sub-souls. Nothing better than cinnabar was found as equal to red blood and consequently no attempts were made to further improve upon sulphur and mercury as the two elements which enter in the make-up of all metals. To accept the redness of cinnabar as soul is to understand mineral magic and to accept sulphur and mercury as sub-souls is to understand alchemy as a phase of mineral magic. Now wherever there was a conception of soul, which is life-essence, there was automatically the power of growth. If plants could donate their soul to increase the life-span of man, minerals, specially red, could do the same. This easily explains how mercurials, or products derived from cinnabar, could do likewise. This theory has persisted upto date for in India vermilion, as Makara Dhwaja, is believed to be a panacea or a drug that reconditions the patient as a whole, rather than specifically remove any particular ailment. so that the one chronically ill becomes healthy and the old becomes young. The drug is all-changing, forcing every indolent tissue to grow and repair itself.

We have however seen that the Chinese represent their immortals carrying as insignia three items, a mushroom, a leaf representing a plant, and a gourd as the container of pills of immortality, otherwise depicted as a red-pill obviously of vermilion. Thus when drugs of rejuvenation, as produce of China, reached Alexandria they were of a mixed nature. We find something similar in Indo-Pakistan where street vendors of such drugs sell them on pavements. Similar must have been the case in ancient Alexandria. As soon as Alexandria became a popular centre of trade, the neighbouring Arab sailors brought Chinese silk for sale. They also brought alchemical drugs of immortality called Kimiya. The poor Arabs did not know what the word signified but they knew the claims as reconditioning the human system, conferring eternal youth and transforming base metals into Ferment-gold, ever-lasting and ever-growing. In Chinese, Kimiya is gold-making juice which signified juice as soul making its acceptor as ever-lasting as gold. The term would however belong to herbal magic. Later on Kimiya was replaced by the term Iksir in Arabic which incorporates the notion of soul as such. Here mineral magic must have superseded. Kimiya in Arabic is identical with Iksir both substances as magical as blood in the eyes of primitive folks. From Read (70; 24) we learn that, as Roger Bacon maintains, "alchemy is a science teaching to make certain medicine called Elixir (Kimiya) which cast upon metals (as) imperfectly (grown) bodies fully perfects them" when their adolescence means their becoming Ferment-gold, ever-growing and hence also ever-lasting. Davis (38; 330) also confirms that according to the same Roger Bacon, "the mineral substances in the mines are quick silver and sulphur; metals and mineral substances are procreated from these". Again from Read (70; 304) we find that given sulphur and mercury they make "baser metals grow and increase", thus imparting the properties of living bodies as bound to make them remain for ever. Elixir prepared from cinnabar comprised of mercury and sulphur, each in its nascent or activated condition, which can then induce any vehicle, man or base metal, to grow and repair to its maximum. It is the resultant of such induced continual growth that can repair itself in every way, appearing in one case as immortal man, and in the other as alchemical gold.

Then alchemical preparations as drugs of immortality and more so of rejuvenation appealed to human nature and the lay Copts of Alexandria must have accepted them for their face value. Alexandria was founded about 300 B.C. By 200 B.C. it had increased in importance for the neighbouring Arab sailors to carry Chinese silk for the Alexandrian market. At the same time they introduced Chinese drugs called Kimiya. They did not know what the word signified so that the Copts also remained ignorant of its sense. Nevertheless Kimiya was transliterated correctly by Bucharic speaking Copts into Greek making Kimiya=Chemeia, the latter pronounced exactly as Kimiya. We picture the importation of Kimiya through the agency of Arab sailors who first handed it over to Copts, both belonging to the lower class of society.

Later when Alexandria became even more famous, Indian merchants went there and also took their Rasayana drugs which again claimed rejuvenation as was the case with Kimiya. Now the Indian merchants could contact the more intelligent Greeks who were familiar by then with Kimiya as drug. The Arabs and Copts both retained Kimiya-Chemeia as loan word, but the Greeks, knowing Indian themselves, could translate Rasayana as Chumeia. Gildemeister has independently etymologized Chumeia as the "Vehicle of Juice" and Rasayana means nothing else. The Arabs went earlier to Alexandria and the Indians came after them. This explains how Chemeia is the older word in Greek than Chumeia and also how the latter as translation is a clear Greek word while the former as loan word connotes nothing in Arabic or in Greek. Then we can fix the birth of the word Chumeia at about 100 A.D., or two hundred years later than that of Chemeia, for both to have been in use as synonyms by about 300 A. D. in Greek. When we realize that as late as about 1000 A. D. Alberuni does not speak of any mercurial alchemy in India, itself it is inconceivable that about 100 A.D. Rasayana could have represented any mercurial or even herbo-mercurial preparation at Alexandria. This came to be the case in India later than 1000 A.D. and it is to this stage that Sir P.C. Ray (29; 80) can refer as follws: "Later on Rasayana was almost exclusively applied to the employment of mercury and other metals in India and at present it means alchemy".

That Chinese silk was being used in Alexandria shows Arabs having brought it all the way from China. With regard to Indians bringing their Rasayanas now needs our attention. Gordon (71; 37) writes that, "the earliest appearance of Indians in Egypt is during the reign of Ptolemy Philadelphus. Asoka had sent an embassy and Buddhist missionaries, with 250 B.C. as the earliest reasonable date. But the dates covering the period of greatest trade activity between the West and India are from the time of Augustus (29 B.C.) to that of Vitellius (69 A.D.)". Indian Rasayanas then could only have been popular about 100 A.D., when we assume Rasayana was translated as Chumeia. There is no doubt that Rasayana, though claiming rejuvenation, was not mercurial. It was either purely herbal or herbo-metallic as with Charaka. That herbal magic was improved upon by mineral magic has been maintained above. Correspondingly herbal Rasayanas were developed into herbo-metallic preparations never ignoring the herbal principle. This is also confirmed by the earliest reference to alchemy in Greek literature itself. Taylor (1; 58) informs that, "the earliest text, pertaining to Greek alchemy, comprises of only a few pages, entitled Gold - making of Cleopatra. The dialogue opens with the words: Cleopatra said to the philosophers (the alchemists): look at the nature of plants" in the first instance. And we know from the rehearsal of the idealized method of making gold as reported by Mukand Singh that the success depends upon the procurement of a gold-making herb. The herb-made gold and alchemical gold made the aged young.

Finally, the Chinese themselves came with their silk to Alexandria. Using their own word Kimiya they could enable later Greeks to translate it as Chrusozomion. Waley (49; 12) writes that Kimiya "Gold-Juice (the Chinese expression) exactly corresponds to Chrusozomion of Zosimus". Thus there were three synonyms in Greek, Chemeia, a loan word directly taken from Arabs, of Chinese origin, Chumeia a translation from the Sanskrit Rasayana and Chrusozomion directly translated from the Chinese with those visiting Alexandria about 200 A. D. Once we assume cinnabar is soul or as red as blood, it explains how "mercurial magic" superseded all "herbal magic". But before mercurials became popular, herbs alone were preferred. Thus even in early Alexandrian alchemy no metals, gold or mercury are mentioned in the first instance but instead plants. All this is in full harmony with the present attitude of accepting alchemy as an offshoot of herbalism. Thus early Alexandrian alchemy was as herbal as early Indian alchemy or even that of China.

Later, even in India mercurials as drugs of rejuvenation were specifically called "the Rasayanas", whereas the previous herbo-mineral preparations, or calcined metals, were renamed Bhasmas or "Burnt". It is this stage then that deserves the remark of Sir P. C. Ray (on p. 80) that "later on Rasayana was almost exclusively applied to the employment of mercury and other metals in medicine and at present it also means alchemy". To be definite, Rasayana means a drug of rejuvenation and a panacea but Rasayanas as medicaments at present are all mercurials, on the other hand non-mercurials are Bhasmas. Rasayana as art continues as before to be concerned with rejuvenation. In as much as they accepted alchemy also as the art of rejuvenation there was no need to coin another name for alchemy. Thus mercurial alchemy and herbal and herbo-metallic Rasayana all became identical in aim when Alchemy=Rasayana.

Finally, it must be pointed out that the idea of rejuvenation has been most ancient and universal. Even the Old Testament speaks of "his flesh as a child's, he shall return to the days of his youth" Job. 39 : 25 "And thy youth shall be renewed like the eagle's" p. 103 : 5. Rejuvenation by incantation, magic, mineral waters, and herbs has been tried all over. Calcined metals as drugs of rejuvenation have been the speciality of India whereas mercurials as that of China. Alchemy can be defined as the art of rejuvenation by means of mercurials as drugs. Both the systems—Indian and Chinese—were offshoots of herbalism.

42. Rasayana as a proper name.

Writers have mentioned princes being interested in alchemy. Alchemy in its degenerate phase as making bullion gold appeals to greedy people, and princes were no exceptions. But let us consider a normal prosperous man enjoying all the comforts and pleasures of life the world can offer. His only anxiety then would be to maintain robust health or youth and next longevity. Here the aims would be identical with those of the ascetic who founded Rasayana in India and alchemy in China. Then to such a prince facing the infirmities of old age his court-physician could not make himself more popular than by specializing in rejuvenation. Now the art of rejuvenation, which is Rasayana, when personified, would be Dr. Rasayana. That Rasayana actually exists as a proper name has been totally ignored. P.C. Ray (29; p. L11) quotes from an old Indian history, the poet Bana's account of the court of King Harsha, who ruled at Kanauj from 605 to 647 A.D., entitled, Harsha-Charita. We are told that there was "a young doctor of Punarvasu race named Rasayana, holding a hereditary position in the royal household". We now proceed directly with the etymology of the name Rasayana. Comparative etymology suggests its comparison with the name Narayana. Mitra's dictionary (66) analyses Narayana with Nara=Water, and Ayana=Shelter. This makes Narayana=Water-Shelter or Water-Protector, which is absurd. But Abdul Hamid (72), in a Bengali textbook, equates Jal=Water=Life. And in dealing with Fountain of Life, we have accepted Water=Life-essence. Accordingly, Narayana = Water-Protector = Life-Protector, and we know otherwise that Narayana=Vishnu, god, the Protector of life. Thus we are sure of our etymology above as correct. After this monograph was completed I incidentally read in K. Bharata Iyer's (107) "Indian Art", Asia Publishing House, Bombay, 1958, p. 31, as follows: "Water is a life-bestowing, sustaining and fertilizing substance and therefore it remains the emblem of life. There are many personifications of the life-giving powers of Water of which Vishnu himself as Narayana, is the Chief".

But whereas Nara = Water, Rasa = Juice. However we have seen that water is the element which created the universe and was the first to have existed. And juice is correspondingly life of the organic world where plants constitute the dominant phase. Thus if Narayana = Water-Protector = Life-Protector then Rasayana = Juice-Protector = Life-Protector. There is nevertheless a difference between the two protectors of life traceable to water as the creative element of the universe and to juice as that of the organic world. Juice, as content, has plant as the container, so that juice-protector is protector of plant life and thus the Sovereign of the vegetable kingdom. There is still another way of looking at the two protectors. The water-protector, as Water-god, evolves into Sun-god, not vice versa. The juice-protector, as god-of-vegetation, becomes Moon-god, next in importance to Sun-god. Now the Sun-god is Vishnu, and Moon-god is Shiva. Whereas Soma, as god, was in charge of vegetation on earth there was the Moon-god, as over-lord of all vegetation, including that on moon, where the choicest herbs grow. Shiva as directly connected with a "Universal herbalism" is traceable to a stage, as Mrs. Bhushan (73; 17) informs that, "Old Bengali literature abounds in references to cotton cultivation. The god Shiva is described as a cultivator of cotton and food grains". Thus providing food and clothing Shiva thereby proves to be an efficient life-protector. With such a past, Shiva acquired suzerainty over herbalism, and as such also over Rasayanas or herbo-metallic preparations, and finally over mercurials, when these became Rasayanas proper. Moreover alchemy is also recognized as Hermetic art for which no proper explanation has been forthcoming. Hermes was the Moon-god of Greece as Siecke (74) has established. Like Shiva, Hermes, as Moon-god, rules over herbalism and thus also over alchemy, which branched off from herbalism. Briefly, the Indian Moon-god, Shiva, gave all three, Herbalism, Rasayana, and Alchemy, while the Greek Moon-god, Hermes, gave Hermetical art, with all preceding stages antecedent to it, implied but not revealed, by authorities on Hermetical Art.

We are still left to show how the Sun-god, Vishnu, is a life-protector as also the Moon-god, Shiva. Quotation from Mrs. Bhushan shows how in the earliest phase Shiva provided food and clothing as befitting a life-protector. But later he was recognized as the destroyer. This however is half the truth. Shiva destroys life mortal to resurrect life immortal. To be an immortalizer he has to be a resurrector and as such a destroyer of mortality. He is really destroyer-cum-resurrector. Some impressed by what occurs first find him to be destroyer, those who await the result recognize him properly as resurrector. Thus by now we can affirm that Vishnu created life mortal, whereas Shiva resurrected it as life immortal. Vishnu tries to protect mortal life, merely prolonging it, Shiva succeeds in conferring immortal life. In popular Hinduism Shiva, not Vishnu, is personified as "the Immortal". And there is no way to immortality-cum-rejuvenation unless there be destruction of what is obviously mortal. Hence Shiva is destroyer first and resurrector next. Correspondingly Rasayana, as the art of rejuvenation, also implies some kind of resurrection without which there can be no reconditioning of a decrepit old system to be transformed into a state of blooming health. We can thus conclude that Rasayana, the art of rejuvenation-cum-immortality, when personified, becomes a synonym of Shiva.

We got so far as to equate Rasayana = Juice-protector = Moon-god = Shiva = Resurrector-cum-rejuvenator. And when Rasayana = Shiva, Dr.

Rasayana of Harsha's court can be renamed Dr. Shiva, and that he was actually called Rasayana has been documented. But by now our interest has been shifted to the personality of Shiva in as much as he is the supreme being to personify rejuvenation. What then is the evolution of Shiva in the light of the history of the pseudo-art of rejuvenation?

43. Rasayana as Shiva, the resurrector, in the Hindu Trinity.

We have Rasayana personified as Dr. Rasayana. further we find Rasayana deified as the god Shiva. To appreciate this we consider the equation, Rasayana = Rejuvenator, and then show that Shiva's career centres round the metamorphosis of an infirm old ascetic into a youth with robust health. Mrs. Bhushan explains Shiva was originally a cultivator-cum-protector offering food and clothing. From a mere protector he became a resurrector and as such a god equal to Vishnu and Brahma. Such an evolution is not strange in Hinduism. Max Muller has shown how the kitchen-fire of the nomad Aryans finally became the powerful god Agni of Vedic religion. Correspondingly Rasayana, the drug of rejuvenation, became Shiva as the deification of the art of rejuvenation. Here I am reminded of what a French cynic has remarked: First man created God in human image, then God created man in divine image. Some tactless people have made direct claim to be gods which was looked upon as apostasy. But to be created "image of god" is practically as good and such a theory got currency. We also learn from Cicero that the licentious Romans made their god voluptuous to justify their own immorality. A similar evolution starts with the art of rejuvenation sublimating it as virtues assigned to a deity. As a result Shiva becomes a rejuvenator and resurrector when he appears as indispensable as Brahma and Vishnu. It is clear that Rasayana was projected to create Shiva and as quoted by P.C. Ray (29; 116) according to popular belief "the science of mercury was communicated by Shiva himself". Briefly, Rasayana first created Shiva and then Shiva created alchemy.

Prof. Nilakanta Sastri (75; 64, 65) writes that, "the name Shiva hardly occurs in Rig Veda as a proper noun. It is applied to many gods of the pantheon in the sense of propitious and once indeed to Rudra himself... Rudra is the father of Maruts and identical with Agni, Fire ... Shiva as the name of a deity is unknown to the ancient Vedic hymns though they mention a tribe of Shivas. The worshippers of the Linga, Phallus, the chief emblem of Shivaism, are condemned in Rig Veda ... Phallic cult with which Shivaism, is connected was wide spread in pre-Vedic India". Thus Shiva and Phallus worship existed in pre-Aryan India and was later adopted into Aryan-Hinduism with Shiva as the resurrector and one of the three foremost gods. Now what is most important is the fact that, "the earliest mention of Shiva worship that can be dated definitely is that of Megasthenes", which brings us to historical times. It leaves us in no doubt that Shiva's position in the Aryan-Hindu pantheon is a very late one.

Rasayana as the division of medicine, and as more important than curative medicine itself, was the conception of ascetics. Shiva in the first instance was an ascetic, and more, the lord of ascetics. As an ascetic-beggar carrying a begging-bowl he is depicted in many a piece of sculpture as also shown by Agrawala (76; facing p. 167). Thus we first identify Shiva = Ascetic.

Now all ascetics were old people. And Shiva as a decrepit old man approached the sage of Himalayas for the hand of his young and beautiful daughter, Parvati. The sage naturally ridiculed the proposal but his daughter nevertheless gave her consent. Shiva then regained his youth and fig. 1 shows him with his wife as ideal young couple. Here Shiva = the Rejuvenated. Because of his successful rejuvenation he was so much envied by other ascetics, naturally all aged, that Shiva became their ideal and lord. This was the outcome of his mastery over herbalism and this in turn was due to his having been the Moon-god. As his insignia he wears in fig. 1 taken from Coomaraswamy (77), the crescent, as the only item of his head dress or crown. As master of herbalism he was able to rejuvenate himself. We note that Shiva wears not only a crescent but also carries a serpent entwining his body. Living underground the serpent is a terrestrial emblem. When Dualism divided Cosmos into two subdivisions, these became Heaven-Earth which had for their synonyms Sun/Moon. Thus Heaven = Sun and Earth = Moon. Whereas Brahma and Vishnu were celestial and solar gods respectively, Shiva was terrestrial-cum-lunar. Thus the Moon-god came to have terrestrial serpent as his emblem. Now the serpent moults annually and was conceived on that ground to renew its youth. Thompson (78; 119) informs that, according to "the Egyptian Book of the Dead, the deceased prays to become like the serpent: I am the serpent Sata. I die and am born again. The Phoenicians believed that the serpent has the faculty not only of putting off old age and renewing its youth but also of increasing its strength and structure". Shiva, who regained his youth and enters the Hindu Trinity as the Resurrector, could not have a better emblem than the serpent as depicted above. Moreover the earth has a soul and this confers fertility. Then who can harbour it better than the serpent, a typical terrestrial creature. Thus the power appearing as fertility in the form of profuse vegetation is that of terrestrial soul and serpent is its custodian. Serpent is thus an emblem both of fertility and of rejuvenation. As such crescent moon on Shiva's head and serpent around his body symbolize the rejuvenating powers of herbs in the moon, as also those of the earth.

Fig. 2 shows Shiva actually filtering a herbal extract as the Rasayana of his choice. What was Soma to Vedic ascetics was Rasayana to post-Vedic Shiva. The scene depicts as if *Cannabis indica* extract and no Soma-juice was the drug. Parvati is helping her husband in the operation of filtration. The scene comes from an old Kashmir (79) enamel. Now enamelling is not indigenous to India so that the art must have been introduced into India from China along with alchemy and Tantrics. This refers to the time when in Kashmir a special school of Shivaism was dominant which dates about 6th Cent. A. D. Maharaja of Kashmir is respectfully awaiting any orders to be carried out. A bull is also shown and bull is the emblem of fecundity associated with Phallus worship. Thus fig. 2 shows Shiva as the lord of herbalism and as such exploiting his knowledge to rejuvenate himself. Meanwhile differentiating the two emblems, Bull and Serpent, Bull = Fecundity or Reproductivity, whereas Serpent = Fertility, being an Earth-Spirit. Moreover the serpent can rejuvenate itself and remain immortal which explains its worship in Southern India by the Shivites and by ancient Egyptians and many others the world over. Briefly, as emblem Serpent = Fertility-cum-Reproductivity = Immortality. And each, Fertility and Reproductivity, is an incarnation of Creative Power. We realize this best by the symbols to which such creative powers are indirectly attributed. Crocodile, as emblem of water, is one, serpent as emblem of terrestrial power, is another. With these two symbols as representing creative powers even delayed rains can be invited as we shall see a little later.

Returning to Shiva as the rejuvenator using herbal extracts in fig. 3, he appears as master-herbalist. Shiva is depicted on a plaque discovered by Agrawala (76; 169) at Ahichchatra, a famous site in India. He has four hands. The left hand in the rear carries a pot of herbs. It becomes the emblem of herbalism. He also wears a broad ribbon, diagonally placed on his body, resting on his left shoulder. It carries, as symbol, a leaf, shown in clear outline. The leaf thus duplicates the herb in the pot. Then his right hand in the rear bears a lotus flower which is quite obvious. Close to it is a circular object clearly beaded. This has been misinterpreted as "a rosary in the back right hand". When a rosary is lifted up it cannot remain circular. Sohoni (80; p. 37) explains that, "the beaded borders on Gupta coins are a row of lotus seeds". The so-called rosary, in fig. 3, is also beaded and would represent lotus seeds. Thus Shiva is holding a lotus flower and a row of lotus seeds. We now come to the importance of lotus itself.

Lotus is the only plant which does not eject its seeds as such to germinate elsewhere. Its seeds mature within the seed-bud and when just germinated leave the mother plant as young living plants. It is the only plant which can be called as it were "ovo-viviparous". This is really a zoological term suggesting that eggs hatch within the mother insect and the young emerge as independent motile creatures. Thus lotus represents the only case of self-generation, as it were, in the plant kingdom. And what is self-generating really means self-reproducing, besides self-growing, which is the feature of all plants. Thus the lotus alone incorporates fertility-cum-fecundity or growth-cum-reproduction; no other plant does this. This makes Lotus a favourite symbol.

By now we should recapitulate the important points discussed. Shiva was primarily an ascetic. He married as an old man. He rejuvenated himself. This achievement is due to his having been Moon-god or lord of herbalism, exploiting herbs on earth and growing even in the moon. He is depicted as a beggar-ascetic, also as the young husband of Parvati. He is a drug-addict, addiction as maintaining rejuvenation and immortality. The snake he carries is an ideal symbol of rejuvenation-cum-immortality. As Moon-god he bears a crescent and Moon-god rules over the herbal kingdom. Another emblem of Shiva is the bull which symbolizes fecundity or virility, a necessary attribute of the rejuvenated. Then a pot of herbs easily duplicates his being recognized as master of herbalism. And lotus symbolizes growth-plus-reproduction, or fertility-plus-fecundity. Thus every emblem of Shiva incorporates reproductive power or rejuvenating power, the two being synonymous.

Rasayana was a drug conceived and tried upon themselves by the aged ascetics. Shiva was the lord of ascetics, himself a drug-rejuvenated hero. He therefore became the rejuvenator-general which means he further became immortalizer and resurrector, for Rejuvenation, Immortality and Resurrection are the same, to have one is to have the others. The means which Shiva adopted was obviously the use of Rasayana drugs. He therefore personifies Rasayana. Moreover as resurrector-cum-immortalizer he has a place in the Trinity. Brahma initiated growth, which means creation; Vishnu preserved life already created but protected life which was mortal; Shiva rejuvenated the aged, resurrected the dead and protected life-immortal. Thus Shiva personifies immortality and as such has a due place in the Hindu Trinity. However this conception must be a late one, certainly post-Vedic.

44. Mercurials as drugs of choice in acquiring rejuvenation.

We have seen such agencies were rich in soul-content, if not even Soul-incorporate; water was soul universal, juice soul of the organic world, blood of the human system, and cinnabar of mineral forms. Now none of these can be fractionated into any constituent excepting cinnabar, which yields its sub-souls, as sulphur and mercury. Many follow the older view giving preference to mercury over sulphur. In the work Rasaratnaker of Nagarjuna, as quoted by Prof. P. Ray (11; 131 and 314), "Darda (or cinnabar) distilled yields an Essence identical with mercury". Now the word for Essence in the text is Satva, which Monier-Williams (31; 1135) translates as, Vital Breath, Essence. And words meaning soul in many languages are derivatives from roots meaning Breath. The Chinese word Ch'i is also primarily Breath, but best connotes Soul. Then Satva=Essence=Soul=Elixir. Moreover Prof. P. Ray (11; 132) quotes verses meaning that, "by partaking of this Elixir (mercury) the body is not liable to decay" and remains in robust health as in youth. Again (on p. 133 and p. 318) we read that, "having prepared with great care the power of projection (it can) transform ten million times in weight of the base metal into gold". It has often been debated if Elixir was a powder or a liquid. Its designation in Sanskrit, is Maharasa, literally the great juice, but clearly denoting mercury, which being a mercurial or a preparation of mercury must be a powder. Recalling our previous interpretation: Rasa=Juice=Soul, it makes Maharasa=Greater Juice=Greater Soul=Elixir, thereby bringing gold-making juice and gold-making mercurials close to each other. When Maharasa=Satva and the latter means Breath or Soul, Maharasa can only signify Greater Soul as more powerful than herbal soul. Accordingly (on p. 161) we read that, the alchemist, Gopal Krishna, "assigns a minor place to the ancient Ayurvedic treatment by Kashaya Yoga i.e. by herbs and Simples", now giving priority to mercurials. And this is because mercurials constituted of Sulphur. and Mercury are dual-natured products, as a hermaphrodite, which is autonomous, needing no partner in becoming productive. Herbs as Simples carry a large quantum of soul, which being mono-elemental, is not capable of self-generation or self-increase. But the hermaphrodite, as self-reproductive, becomes creative, and equating Reproduction=Creation we get the Hermaphrodite=Creator. We have symbols to confirm such to have been the conception while they were designed. Now what is a hermaphrodite by constitution is a ferment by function. And to the alchemist the ideal ferment was Ferment-gold, ever-increasing being a ferment and ever-lasting in form being gold. When this is taken as a drug it makes the human system grow for ever but normally repairing all defects due to disease or age. Base metals would also grow to perfection which means as fire-proof gold. Thus the alchemist identified Ferment-gold=Hermaphrodite=Immortalizer. And the precursor of Ferment-gold was the Mercury/Sulphur preparation, or Elixir, or Rasayana which could permeate into the system of its acceptor, be it man or metal, and make it grow to perfection or become ever-lasting. To such a powerful mercurial Rasayana was given the highly complimentary designation, Makara Dhwaja.

Makara Dhwaja signifies Emblem of Makara. Makara is a fabulous creature, its anterior half resembles crocodile, its posterior half fish. Makara then is half fish and half crocodile, both aquatic animals. Water, as the universal life-essence and the primordial element, is the greatest creative power. Moreover we can recall Pagel's (81) observation that accordingly "water creatures symbolize stages in the transformation both of humid matter outside and blood-bound soul inside". With matter and blood-soul together a life form must result, and this is expected from the powers assigned to water. Since the origin of life and body is one, both arising from water, the resultant must be Soul-incorporate. Had there been a separate soul it would take a body of different origin and their union would be a reincarnation. But body and soul emanating from the same source we get a Soul-incorporate, body being soul or soul identical with the body. Such is also Resurrection Body, unlike Reincarnation Body, the latter capable of dissolution, whereas the former inseparable. A Soul-incorporate diffusing into another system, sublimates the corporeal nature of the acceptor, and makes it soul-like. The transformation produces another Soul-incorporate, with powers physical and spiritual characterizing a super-man. What is Aladin's lamp as a domestic article is Soul-incorporate as a drug, and correspondingly the mercurial-made immortal among men. The final super-man carries a Resurrection Body knowing no space and no death, virtues best known as characterizing the personality of Jesus after his resurrection.

Having discussed what idealized aquatic life forms can signify we turn first to fish as half of Makara. Fish is the one creature which best illustrates multiplicity and most qualified to represent reproductivity. The Cod for example is known to lay over a million eggs at a time. And what is so prolific assures itself of its perpetuity but this is true of the species rather than of the individual. However the individual is also a member of the species and as such its representative. Thus as far as reproductivity is concerned, Reproduction=Immortality. This increases the series of equivalents including Immortality when, Rejuvenation=Immortality=Resurrection=Reproductivity. Fortunately the symbolism of fish has been well studied; it exists also in Christian art where it serves as the emblem of Jesus, both as immortals.

Let us here attempt to understand creation. It is something inconceivable for it assumes existence with nothing preceding it. Now man observed that growth of a plant depends at least upon water and that of an animal upon food. On the contrary reproduction appears to be independent of foreign provision, it is production out of the resources of the system itself. Thus reproduction comes nearest to creation as production out of nothing other than the system itself. From such reasoning man equated Reproduction=Creation.

This also explains the philosophy supporting Shivaism. Reproductive power being creative power, the male reproductive organ became the symbol also of creative power and as such Linga or Phallus came to be worshipped. Nilakanta Sastri (75; 98) explains that, in "Shivaism, Phallus worship is worship of the Creative Cosmic principle", and that the "Linga or Phallus (becomes) Divinity (or Creativeness) concretely present". All such notions are directly attributable to Reproduction=Creation. Thus when we come to a hermaphrodite it is self-growing, which does not mean much, but it is also self-reproducing and as such creative. Now a ferment is also self-reproductive and when gold, already ever-lasting, becomes self-reproductive it becomes creative power ever-lasting. This makes Gold-ferment the best of its kind. Accordingly the alchemist equated Hermaphrodite = Ferment = Immortalizer. The Christian alchemist has further substituted as symbols Jesus = Ferment = Immortalizer and also Hermaphrodite = Creator. In as much as fish is a prolific breeder it functions like a hermaphrodite. However Makara Dhwaja is more than fish.

We have now to deal with Makara, the Sanskrit word for crocodile. Flowing water is most obvious as rivers and the largest creature found therein is the crocodile. This is true of most large rivers the world over. Then crocodile becomes the emblem of water and as such symbolizes the life-giving powers, both as Fertility and Fecundity. To remind again, Fish, another emblem of water, represents Reproductivity, rather than growth. Archaeologists have already studied crocodile as symbol. Mallowan (82; 120) refers to "a seal in Egypt from Osiris temple identical with lizard (design found in Mesopotamia at Brak) described by Petrie as crocodiles ... These lizard (crocodile) designs in Egyptian seals and elsewhere may be connected with the act of reproduction". Thus both Fish and Crocodile serve as symbols of Fecundity or Reproductivity which has to be further equated with creative power. Now this can also be confirmed. In some villages of India (as in Maharashtra) a procession would be instituted to invite rain. Besides the cobras in pots there would be carried on long poles the giant monitor lizard in lieu of the crocodile. The lizard would be further smeared with vermilion as though it was being consecrated with Redness as soul to represent it as the plenipotentiary of the creator. Here the lizard is the proper substitute of a crocodile for the lizard is carried alive and later allowed to escape as such. Then the reptile first represents crocodile and as such reproductivity or creative powers which can easily induce rainfall. And it has been explained that a serpent also represents Fertility. The interested reader may refer to the article by H. Miller (83; 460) who also illustrates the lizard.

There is a parallel case more obvious, as appeal to reproductive power in conferring fertility. Crawford (84) reproduces a picture showing, in a farm, "Phallic menhirs near Soddu in South Ethiopia" so that the cultivator believed, to have the symbol of the generative organ was as good as having reproductive power itself, and once reproductivity was there, fertility was bound to be present as well. This custom of erecting the image of Phallus would also explain Shivaism. The power that the Phallic menhir would generate would be creative power which is what Shiva worshipper of the same symbol also believes, and which he uses as the main object of worship. Theoretically Phallus, incorporating reproductive powers, is endowed with creative powers, and as such becomes the emblem of the creator himself. Nilakanta Sastri actually states that in Shivaism "Linga (Phallus) is Divinity concretely present". It is as good as the plenipotentiary of the creator. It seems a highly exaggerated idea but facts conspire to confirm such belief. Returning to Makara, the Crocodile more than the Fish, was Fertility-cum-

Fecundity, and being Fish and Crocodile it represents the ideal combination of reproductive-cum-creative powers. Das Gupta (85; 43) found "a temple frieze depicting Makara. Its body became a geometric pattern (as an ever-increasing spiral). Its head resembles that of an alligator (or crocodile) and from its open jaws springs a creeper (which is a plant with a spiral body). This motif is a fertility symbol and common to early Indian art". The body itself as spiral, further emitting a creeper as spiral from the mouth, suggests that spirals symbolize growth, which is ideal as characterizing a creeper. It means Makara here has transformed its reproductive power of fecundity into vegetable growth or Fertility. The Phallic menhirs of Ethiopia would likewise produce fertility though they essentially symbolize fecundity.

Having dealt with Makara we return to Makara Dhwaja, the Emblem of Makara, which is cinnabar or mercuric sulphide. Symbolizing the virtues of fish and crocodile these represent reproductive-cum-creative powers. As actually prepared sulphur is taken with mercury to which gold is added and the mixture sublimated. The resultant is vermilion with traces of gold. It is pulverized and further levigated or made fine enough to become soul-like. This refined form is called Anu-Makaradhwaja or "atomized" Vermilion which becomes the best panacea recognized in Indian medicine; only next comes calcined gold on which the Maharaja of Gondal (45; 139) correspondingly writes that, "it is said to be a cure of nearly all diseases (and) removes the effects of old age and restores the vigour of manhood. It is stimulant and aphrodisiac". Makara Dhwaja being the drug par excellence in this sense was called the Emblem of Makara.

Fig. 4 shows Makara, with a crocodile's head bearing horns and its body ending in a tail as that of a fish. What is interesting is the duplication of its powers of fecundity revealed by a semi-nude sex-appealing young woman, holding a child to confirm her being by no means sterile. Since a symbol of reproductivity also becomes a symbol of immortality, Makara is found even on churches in Europe. Fig. 4 however is taken from Marshall's (86) work on Gandhara Art.

45. Makara Dhwaja or Cupid's Hallmark.

Following Goethe's instruction we tried first to interpret Rasayana = Elixir and thereby to compare Rasayana or "Indian geriatrics" with Chinese alchemy. Makara Dhwaja is now to be translated not literally but rendered effectively to bring out the sense it incorporated when the term was coined. Makara Dhwaja is a panacea and also an aphrodisiac. We have seen how on taking Rasayanas old sages became "attractive to women". Makara, itself symbolizes reproductive power and Makara Dhwaja is its emblem. Thus Makara Dhwaja as drug should also be an aphrodisiac which would imply this as its crowning virtue. Now in Greek mythology Cupid is the god of love and as such would be most interested in aphrodisiacs. Then a preparation after his heart, to meet with his approval, can be called Cupid's Emblem. Here we have merely replaced Makara by Cupid, but we can proceed to confirm the rendering Cupid's Emblem. Fig. 5 is taken from Read (87) and shows a laboratory where Cupids are the alchemists. When they have approved of the quality of their preparation this would naturally bear "Cupid's Hallmark" which would correspond to Makara Dhwaja of Indian pharmacy, earlier translated as Makara's Emblem. Of the two designations for a drug, "Cupid's Hallmark" is more appropriate than Cupid's Emblem. Fig. 5 represents a painting of a European artist who has fully realized that alchemical drugs also claim aphrodisiac properties. Properly speaking they are more than rejuvenating drugs, making one "young and attractive to women" as a regular Cupid.

46. Mercury as related to Shiva in Indian mythology.

We further wish to confirm Makara Dhwaja = Cupid's Hallmark. We replace Cupid by Shiva as the god of the art of rejuvenation-cum-immortality. He would then personify mercurials as the drug of choice for rejuvenation. We have seen that the one power which is present in all such drugs is that of soul, a real creative power. Now Indian cosmogonists have otherwise conceived five cosmic elements together representing creative powers responsible for the existence of the Universe and of everything therein. There is a Tantric text quoted by P.C. Ray (29; 74) which states that, "Mercury (itself) is composed of the five elements (integrating the total creative power) and represents Shiva himself". Here Shiva becomes the creator and mercury the agency he employs. Briefly, Creative powers = Five Cosmic elements = Mercury = Shiva. Moreover another text explains (on p. LXXIII) that, "mercury is produced by the creative (= reproductive) conjunction of Hara (Shiva) and Gauri (Parvati) and mica is produced from Gauri ... Mica (Sulphur) is the seed (of Gauri) and mercury is the seed of Hara." Instead of the original Chinese elements Lead/Mercury we have Mica/Mercury in early Indian alchemy. The reader here may refer to paragraph 30 for comparison. The text is confusing when we go into details but Mercury, and not Mica, is volatile and mercury is Spirit or the Male principle. When this unites with mica, obviously inert and corporeal, the latter is enlivened. The picture would be similar to the word of God entering a clod of earth and creating a life form where the word, as energy, emanating from the creator is incorporated in matter. But in the above case mercury comes not as energy but as "Prime Matter" as it were, or some part of Shiva, the creator. Mercury conceived as part of the creator becomes creative power. Indian mythology further specifies mercury as Shiva's Semen, when semen is to the forthcoming progeny what "Prime Matter" is to alchemical products. In fact one recognized meaning of Rasa also identifies it as Shiva's Semen. In harmony with such a conception, the alchemist is advised to make "a Phallus of mercury and place it in the East" as quoted by P.C. Ray (29; 117). Phallus is the emblem of procreative-cum-creative power, and mercury, as semen, is its real content, and the nature of the content can be deduced from that of its container and vice versa. This mythological conception of Shiva is clearly a very late invention by Shivites who were the pioneers of alchemy in India.

47. Persistence of herbalism in mercurial alchemy.

The one idea which permeates throughout the contents here is that of a Growth-force and this is herbal in origin. From herbal Rasayanas we finally reach preparations of mercury and sulphur, thereby apparently shutting all doors against herbalism. Now the alchemist who wanted to make gold, always as Ferment-gold, took mercury and tried to make it fire-proof, a property which would best bring it nearest to gold. Once mercury became fire-proof it could be coloured yellow, as it were, to further change it as gold. Now to make mercury fire-proof is to infuse such a powerful soul that it will grow so fast that any injury done to it by heat can be repaired instantaneously. We know a ball can be kept suspended by a jet of water forced from below. Here mercury becomes heat-proof because it is forced to grow fast enough to repair any injury. It is this growth energy which it also offers to a base metal to make it grow to be fire-resistant and thereby gold. P.C. Ray (29; vol. 2, 28) quotes from a Sanskrit work as follows: "Shiva said: I shall reveal a most wonderful mystery. An oil from the bulbous root of a plant rubbed with mercury and calcined gives mercury the property of converting one hundred thousand times its weight of base metal into gold".

The plant donated its power of growth to mercury and this transferring the same to base metals made them grow to perfection which means until they became fire-proof. Really speaking the soul donating agencies or resurrecting agencies, when metals were killed by heat, were plants. This further explains what an Indian classic on alchemy, named Rasaratnasamuchchaya, recommends as P.C. Ray (29; 116) translates a passage from it stating that, "the laboratory is to be erected in a region which abounds in medicinal herbs and wells". Even the earliest text in Greek alchemy points in the first instance to "the nature of plants". Splendor Solis (88; 29), a classic on alchemy in Europe dated 1582, explicitly affirms that "the herb Lunatica or Berissa (with) its roots as metallic Earth, has a red stem, grows easily, and if put in Mercury changes into perfect silver and this again by further decoction changes into gold. And this gold (as a ferment) turns hundred parts of mercury into the finest gold. There is a fable relating that Aeneus and Silvus went to a tree which had golden branches and as often as one broke a branch off another one grew in its place". The legend was added as appealing to human curiosity but it serves to emphasize the nature of active principle with which alchemy is concerned and it is the power of growth, ever-lasting. It will be noticed that Alberuni, Mrs. Postans and Prof. Aga Hyder Hassan all have narrated similar legends. Thereby we note first, that a miraculous herb is exploited and this makes everything grow so well that the acceptor of Growth-soul becomes ever-lasting, be it as Ferment-gold or as immortal man.

48. Shiva as hermaphrodite and creator.

We have not been able so far to explain the origin of creative power which really goes to make man immortal and also change a base metal into an ever-lasting and ever-growing entity as Ferment-gold. We have to recapitulate the development of Animism, Dualism and Monism to be able to realize how we finally get to creative power. The early man as hunter believed in blood as soul which was all powerful. We have the picture of a Jinn in "Arabian Nights" which can be compressed in a pot and made to remain there inert like dead matter as also be freed to prove as powerful as the devil. Aladin's lamp, as a domestic article, was also such a power but as a humble and unimpressive incarnation of soul. In power at least it was identical with a Jinn. In such cases it was the spirit or soul alone that counted. It is moreover to be assumed that the Animist did observe children growing as also trees so that he could equate Growth = Life. Assuming that there is soul, its incarnation would appear as body when existence as body and soul could be easily explained. The Upanishads explain the Universe as the work of the creator who, subsequently, entered into it. It is like saying that energy froze into matter but a trace remained as such and together were looked upon as body and soul. Everything that exists was constituted likewise and even the Universe owed its existence to Cosmic Soul. But Animism could not explain the origin of things or creation of any kind, not even human birth.

When man took to pastoral life, as herdsman, he realized that a male and female pair of animals uniting produced an issue. He further generalized and came to believe that there must be a sort of Adam and Eve for every form of existence, not excluding the Universe. Here the Cosmic progenitors became in Chinese Yang and Yin or the elements of Cosmic Soul. They would be like the two poles of a magnet and it was essential to assume their co-existence from the very beginning. It was however illogical to grant that there were two entities at the very start of creation. Then it would be equally justifiable to assume more. For the sake of consistency the two primordial elements were to be reduced to one. Here begins Monism. We find such an attempt even in the Biblical story of man's creation. Adam and Eve were not born separately. Eve came from a rib of Adam and Adam from a clod of earth. There was thus only one source from which Adam and Eve were born. The Upanishads start with a two-seeded fruit which dividing gave rise to man and woman as the first pair of human beings as twins. In both the theories Dualism is really disguised. On the contrary a boiled egg cut longitudinally can give two as mirror images which would be opposites, yet not identical. Only in such a case we can predict, taking either, what the other as the opposite can be. The case would be the same with a bipolar magnet. If we have one pole we also know what the other must be. Maier (89), a German alchemist, in 1617, offered a symbol placing an egg in an erect position, with the creator lifting a sword to cut the same, naturally longitudinally, when the result must give two mirror images. The picture would correspond to an illustration when a two-seeded fruit is to be cut into its two halves. Such would be the symbolism of Monism. In Animism Soul and Body are really one, like steam and ice, or like energy and matter, when one can change into the other. In Dualism, Soul and Body are no longer inter-changeable. Each has its own sub-elements and these are two. Life then comprised of four elements, two corporeal and two spiritual. Body= Corporeal element donated by the father, plus that contributed by the mother. Life-essence = Spirit, the male Growth-soul plus Soul-specific or "the Soul", the female sub-soul. However the corporeal elements fused into unity were indissoluble so that life consisted of three fractions. Life = Body + Spirit + Soul, when Spirit and Soul existed as a loose mixture. Such an integrated system could not be ever-lasting and accordingly Dualism easily explained how man was mortal for which Animism had no reply. Moreover

Dualism could also suggest how man can acquire immortality. Just as Union of opposites results in procreation or continuity of species, Spirit and Soul fusing into unity would produce an ever-increasing soul when the body can never run out of stock of it and man is bound to live for ever. It means Reproduction was equated with Creation allowing an autonomous entity to increase for ever. Growth is autonomous and explains how Growth = Life. This in turn accounts for Fertility being conceived as immortality and worshipped in many a cult. Whereas Growth seems to have its own limits, reproductivity knows no brake. Thus far more than growth or fertility, reproductivity or fecundity is ever-continuing and if this be the evidence considering the present and the future, the same must be true of the past which then appears as creation. Creation and Reproduction become past and present phases of the same phenomenon. Pre-dated reproduction is creation; post-dated creation is reproduction. Then if growth is life, reproduction is immortal life. And to be able to exist for ever the power has to be creative for which the synonym is "reproductive." This explains how reproductive organs, as the instruments of the powers of reproduction, or the source generating such power, have been looked upon as the source of creative power itself. The male/female sex organs, Lingam/Yoni, jointly constitute an image which is worshipped in Shivaism. Apart from it the Bull, incorporating the virility of the male, is another associated object of worship. In other cults goat and paired serpents are likewise worshipped. Really speaking primitive worship is indirectly worship of life with its two phases: Growth and Reproduction. Sun worship is worship of Growth and here the Vishnuvites lead. The images the Shivites worship pertain to Reproduction as explained above. Now what is not worshipped is pure creation and there are only two or three temples in India dedicated solely to Brahma, whereas there is no scarcity of Shivite and

Vishnuvite temples. Once Reproduction = Creation, to worship as the Shivites do is to worship Creative Power. Remembering that life means both growth and reproduction, worship of Fertility and that of Fecundity get identified. In Hindu religion, correspondingly, these two worships often overlap or run parallel to each other.

The above discussion gives us a clear idea of Dualism and of Monism resulting from it. The joint-images of male/female sex organs would be a symbol of two opposites as one, like a hermaphrodite or like the two poles of a magnet. This idea has been further extended to Shiva himself. Consequently there has resulted an androgynous Shiva. To be one as also the creator he had to be as it were Adam/Eve as half and half. The androgynous Shiva then is another version of the male/female sex organs that are depicted also as a Unit symbol. To interpret two obviously independent entities, two-as-one, there resulted two halves as one.

Fig. 6 is a pen and ink drawing of a 6th Cent. image of Shiva in a temple at Mahakteswar, in the Deccan, taken from Rambach (90) and De Golish. Even in China Yang/Yin constituting the Cosmic Soul, or the source of all existence, have been depicted as Red/Black opposites and as halves of a circular whole. This symbol is very well known and needs a mere reference. Even the Babylonians have depicted an androgynous deity, which is reproduced in Jung and further offered and discussed in an earlier article (91). Moreover the alchemists have also conceived of a hermaphrodite showing King/Queen corresponding to the androgynous Shiva. The best symbol is the design of Jamsthaler who offered it in 1625 and is reproduced here as fig. 7 taken from Jung (92).

49. Shiva as related to Brahma and Vishnu.

In as much as Shiva is popularly accepted as the destroyer, the reader would expect evidence justifying any other interpretation. To put it in simple language when Brahma has been recognized as the Creator what is the position of androgynous Shiva. There is obvious contradiction in admitting Shiva to be a creátor. But a resurrector can only be one who is also a creator. This is the simple answer to the above criticism. Rambach and De Golish (90) quote from Harivamsa text which maintains, "Vishnu is Shiva, Shiva is Brahma, single is the form, three are the gods: Vishnu, Shiva and Brahma. Creators of the world, Protectors of the world, in themselves complete. They are the *Lord who is half woman*" or androgynous. Now it appears that the god that entered the pantheon last became the most powerful of the three. Shiva entered Aryan-Hinduism later than Brahma and Vishnu and has superseded them. Holzmann (93; 198) finds that in Mahabharata Shiva is both under Brahman and over Brahman. We are however in a position to explain how Shiva came to supersede all. Brahma created life and forgot the world. Vishnu is alert and tries to keep the mortal free from miseries and sorrow; he is therefore far more popular than Brahma. Shiva is the resurrector-cum-immortalizer and any one who fears death or aspires for immortality, be it as post-mortem life, must accept Shiva as the foremost. We are here incidentally facing the two popular schools of Hinduism, of Vishnuvites and Shivites, the former realistic praying for longevity, the latter idealistic longing for immortality. The ascetics wanted rejuvenation leading to immortality, hence most alchemists were Shivites. Even Buddhism was essentially allied to Shivaism rather than to Vishnuvism. And the Buddhist alchemists were ascetics and as such further allied to Shivites than to Vishnuvites.

A later acquaintance with Bharata Iyer's (107) book first confirms (on p. 31) that "Brahma is the Creator but creation having been completed he is no longer an active god. His powers were absorbed by

Vishnu and Shiva, whose cults have attained (real) popularity". And the situation is best understood as Aryan-Hinduism trying to assimilate later on non-Aryan deities among whom were all the three gods Brahma, Vishnu and Shiva. Of Shiva we have been duly informed by Nilakanta Sastri (75) in paragraph 43. Iyer (107; 7) would now add that, "in the Vedic period (even) Brahma was not an important deity. Vishnu had hardly emerged, he exists in association with the Sun-god, Surya. Shiva appears to be a later adaptation". All over the pagan world sun finally came to be looked upon as the source of life and virtually the creator. Apparently pre-Aryan India had advanced enough to conceive Brahma, and not the sun, as the creator. As a result the Aryan Sun-god, Surya, was merged into Vishnu who became the Sun-god and then the progenitor of Brahma. Thus Iyer (on p. 31) explains that, "when Vishnu thought of creating the universe a golden lotus stemmed out of his navel and Brahma emerged from this flower. He is called Abja-Yoni, lotus-born, and also Pitamaha, the grandsire of the human race. Lotus as water plant is also a symbol for water as for the primordial waters (which created life as apart from supporting life). Water is the life-bestowing, (life) sustaining and fertilizing substance and therefore remains the emblem of life". In fact Egyptian mythology reveals that the Water-god later becomes the Sun-god, the creator, and not inversely that Sun-god becomes Water-god. Here Vishnu, as Narayana, was Water-god, who later became Sun-god. When he was elevated to this stage of sublimity from him was evolved Brahma as explained by Iyer above. Briefly, Vishnu created Brahma and Brahma created the universe. Brahma is depicted in a piece of sculpture of 7th Cent., now in the Prince of Wales Museum, Bombay, with four heads and four hands". In one, to quote Iyer (p. 32), he "bears a water pot which symbolizes his function as the creator". Really speaking the creator should be Sun-god-cum-Water-god, but in as much as Water-god easily evolves into Sun-god we have here a clear case of Water-god alone as the Creator. Even Vishnu, the Sun-god, reveals his first incarnation as god to be as fish, which cannot but symbolize water, and thereby confirm the origin of Sun-god as Water-god. Then Brahma the creator becomes the prodigy of Vishnu, the Sun-god, who was the Water-god. In other words Water-god becomes the supreme creator or Vishnu over Brahma, which Holzmann also found in Mahabharata. And Iyer (p. 21) explicitly states that, "when the supreme being, Narayana (the Water-god) willed creation, a thousand petalled golden lotus shot up from his navel on which appeared Brahma, charged with the duties of creation". Properly interpreted Vishnu becomes the author-creator while Brahma the executor-creator. Vishnu as Water-god and Sun-god can be easily appreciated as the creator and progenitor of Brahma, the mere executor of already planned creation. Now what should interest us most is the fact pointed out by Iyer (on p. 32) that, "in one of his hands Brahma may be found holding a phial containing the *elixir of life* as befitting his position as the lord of life". We have only to be sure of the nature of this elixir which, as the content of a phial, becomes Water, which we must recognize as Water-of-life. Here we incidentally realize that whatever be the nature of elixir it is a creative element, one which can recondition the entire system, resurrecting if dead, immortalizing if living but mortal.

50. Drugs of longevity versus of immortality.

We have discussed the following drugs as types: Soma or Ephedra juice, herbo-metallic complexes as calcined metals, mercury-sulphur complex, as elixir, and Ferment-gold, the masterpiece among immortalizing drugs. We have to show how they appear in the light of impacts of Animism, Dualism and Monism upon pharmacy. Soma was a juice saturated with soul which was mono-elemental as assumed by Animism and would add to the stock of soul of its consumer much as a dose of vitamin would do every time it is taken. Soma had to be taken daily since the soul was a definite quantum and not ever-increasing. A herbo-metallic complex depended upon Dualism. Its soul was bi-elemental, with sub-souls, as opposites and self-generative, like a hermaphrodite by constitution and ferment by function. A single dose could confer immortality. Calcined gold was the best of its class since gold was already ever-lasting and could easily donate this virtue. Moreover the herbal soul imbibed in the herbo-aurous complex could make the life of its consumer grow like a plant. Monism finally suggested taking the opposites from the same source and re-uniting them to constitute an inseparable unity. Now cinnabar was red lik blood which was soul. Its constituents, sulphur and mercury, were sub-souls. But in cinnabar they were loosely mixed. However when reconditioned to appear at par with each other their resultant became like a hermaphrodite-cum-ferment. It was Elixir, for which the Sanskrit word actually used was Satva. Elixir, like the calcined metal, was a drug which primarily induced its acceptor to grow and then to its maximum, making it ever-lasting. To grow means to be alive and to continue to grow for ever implies immortality. When a base metal became the recipient of such drugs it became a live-metal first and when it reached its limit of growth it became fire-proof as gold. Synthetic gold became Ferment-gold, a living substance. The same made human soul ever-increasing and thereby, never parting from the human body, made man immune to death.

We can compare elixir to lactic acid bacterium and Ferment-gold to curdled milk. A single inoculation of the germs suffices to produce curd and this trans-planted continues to curdle fresh milk. Elixir likewise makes Ferment-gold and this can change base metals into gold as also make man immune to death. It is easy to realize that one can remain in doubt if the bacterium is of the right kind to produce curd and correspondingly if a substance is elixir. On the contrary neither curd nor Ferment-gold can leave us in such doubts as to their virtues. That. is why the alchemist made the preparation of Ferment-gold his target. But alchemy as art reached the stage of perfection in the preparation of elixir, for to further make gold with it was a mere child's play. The existence of sulphur-mercury complex, as elixir, has been implicitly mentioned by van Helmont for he refers to a heavy yellow powder which he inoculated into mercury and changed it into gold. He was a religious-minded renowned scientist during the late medieval ages.

51. The nature of active principle in drugs of immortality.

If we speak of a medicinal plant we must also speak of its active principle. Today Ephedra is the vehicle of Ephedrine. Formerly it was the carrier of a large but fixed quantum of soul, like orange juice being rich in ascorbic acid. In calcined metals and in elixirs, above all, in Ferment-gold, the active principle was a dual-natured soul, male and female sub-souls joined like a hermaphrodite and made self-reproductive like a ferment. We have discussed such a constitution in androgynous Shiva. It means that he was self-creative because he was androgynous and this was the resultant of union of opposites so that importance starts with two elements or two entities as one.

52. Sublimating sub-souls as prelude to union of opposites.

There is no doubt that a metal and a plant are opposites. But it became a difficult art calcining the metal, pulverizing it and finally making it fine enough to become soul-like and the proper counterpart of herbal soul. In practice the art proved difficult. On the contrary sulphur and mercury were opposites like brother and sister born out of the same source. But mercury proved much too motile and had to be transformed into a heat-stable substance. Here we read in Splendor Solis (88; 29) that, "the herb Lunatica or Berissa, has a red stem. If put in Mercury changes itself into perfect Silver" or into a stage, when it is heat-stable. Then mixing mercury previously stabilized with sulphur colours it yellow, producing ever-lasting gold. Here the real art was to treat, as before, mercury, as Soul-corporeal, with a suitable herb. The Growth-soul of the plant introduced into mercury made the latter grow as fast as any injury inflicted upon it with the result that mercury could repair all injuries and retain its form. Such a conception of genuineness existed in earlier times when ordeal by fire was in vogue. In our case a metal capable of growing fast was a self-repairing metal, and accordingly the herbo-mercurial complex remained as fire-proof mercury. Into such "solid mercury" sulphur was introduced which imparting it a yellow colour, made it gold. We must note that in the above experiment most attention was devoted to mercury, the carrier of Soul-corporeal. This feature is common to every art concerned with immortality. The resultant, as immortalizing agent, represents body and soul as one, and for these two to become one, the body had to be made sublime or soul-like. We are here indirectly facing the distinction between Reincarnation Body and Resurrection Body. In a Reincarnation Body, soul and body each remains unchanged. When the soul-content of Soma passed into the system of the consumer, life of man was merely prolonged, the body of the acceptor was not made soul-like and there remained a loose mixture of body and herbal soul. On the contrary a Resurrected Body comprises of a body which, though corporeal, is soul-like, if not even soul. Two unequals make a Reincarnation Body, two equals constitute a Resurrection Body. The latter alone is inseparable being one, hence immortal. Growth-soul and Soul-corporeal as equals give a soul-incorporate, be it an immortalizing drug or an immortal man. Accordingly, we have finally as equivalents, Elixir = Hermaphrodite=Ferment=Soul-incorporate=Resurrection Body.

53. The one origin of creative power.

We have realized that if we have two entities as soul and soul-like body there results union of opposites which is self-increasing. The question arises as to the origin of anything more than one. Logically we can assume only one primordial entity characterizing it with a single property. We therefore start with a quantum of energy and grant that it can expand or grow. Expansion of energy automatically creates a difference of potential and some energy freezes as matter creating a partial vacuum of energy. Then some growth - energy rushes back, produces an impact upon matter, and even penetrates it. This means matter is frozen-energy with a trace of impact-energy or the original growth-energy. This explanation corresponds to the cosmogony propounded in the Upanishads. The creator created the Universe and then entered into it. In our explanation growth-energy is the creator, matter is creation, and the trace of impact-energy in matter can be compared with the creator who has entered his creation. We admit no matter is absolutely free from energy.

Proceeding further with the expansion of matter this explodes due to an excess of imbibed impact-energy as related to the mass of matter. There results explosions and destruction of matter. But again energy freezes and creates matter until some matter incorporates much less impact-energy. At this stage expansion reaches the explosion point due to Growth-soul or impact-energy but the Soul-corporeal as matter puts a check and, instead of explosion into innumerable parts, a division into two takes place. Division results when Growth-soul and Soul-corporeal exist in their right proportion enabling the latter to check the former properly.

The genesis of such multiplicity initiated by the creation of Growth-soul and Soul-corporeal, as opposites emerging from a common source, has its counterpart in Brihadranayaka Upanishad (94; 50). It explains that the Creator (Brahma) assumed the form as Prajapati (as the actual creator) and "became man and wife embracing each other. He divided (such a dual-natured) body into two. Therefore this body of man is one half of himself like the half of a two-celled seed". An improved idea would be that of mirror images which are invariably two and supplementary. It is however easy to see that the Indian theory was created to explain the birth of man and woman like that of Adam and Eve from the same clod of dust. Any one whose common sense is sufficiently strong can see that instead of starting with two primordial entities, the Upanishad starts with a two-celled seed, which is really disguised Dualism. Instead of saying there was an androgynous creator we have a two-seeded fruit which leaves us to wonder as to the origin of such a queer entity. On the contrary we have a theory of cosmogony when an egg cut vertically gives two mirror images as opposites and this has been actually offered as a symbol by the alchemist Maier, though the interpretation given here is not his. Then given two, as Growth-soul and Soul-corporeal, they become opposites and their union Soul-reproductive and multiplicity starts when, Reproduction=Creation. It is however easily seen that to stop with Growth-soul and Soul-corporeai would be Dualism but to trace their origin to Growth-soul would be Monism.

54. Legends implying alchemy as initiating creation.

Legends are treated here as emphasizing features present but not striking enough. They serve like diagrammatic sketches in a scientific treatise. One wonders what an art, supposed to make gold, has to do with creation. Here the first thing to admit is that synthetic gold was a living substance, a ferment first and gold next. Then to create a live ferment is creation proper. Dante lived in an age when alchemy was popular. He had therefore opportunities to realize that alchemy imitated creation and accordingly he placed the alchemist in his Inferno. Now legends unequivocally present alchemy as creating life. Prof. Eis (95) discusses some features of "creative activity" on which alchemy depends. Above all there is "homunculus who originated from human sperm implanted in (some) cucumber". Moreover even long before Paracelsus (1493-1541) "the experimental creation of life in a glass retort was alleged among the alchemists". Such would be a legend based upon the actual claim that alchemical gold as Ferment-gold was a living substance.

55. Dualism versus pantheism and alchemy.

The alchemist has been blamed for being a pantheist and it seems appropriate to absolve him of this charge. Here it is best to distinguish among Animism, Dualism, Monism and Pantheism. This we do to finally show that the ideal preparation can be best interpreted as Resurrection Body and not as Reincarnation Body. Animism recognizes a mono-elemental soul present even among metals and plants. Dualism is an extension of Animism attributing a dual nature to soul. According to Dualism existence began with two entities Yang and Yin, or as androgynous creator which is disguised Dualism. Monism begins with one entity, here called Growth-soul. Growth-energy on freezing gives rise to Soul-corporeal appearing as matter. Thus arises Dualism of energy and matter, of Growth-soul and Soul-corporeal, of creator and creation. It is also obvious that Soul-corporeal or creation contains traces of Growth-soul or, that the present carries some of its past, while the inverse is not correct. There is much Growth-soul free from any trace of Soul-corporeal. Moreover a third possibility also arises. The presence of Growth-soul varies in quantity from case to case in different forms of creation as matter. When the ratio between Soul-corporeal and the incorporated impact Growth-soul is ideal there also results Soul-reproductive, a modified form of Growth-soul. The above statement suggests that when Soul-corporeal contains only traces of Growth-soul, as in a crystal of alum, the entity remains a form of inorganic matter. But when the quantum of Growth-soul is more than traces, Soul-corporeal can exercise a check upon Growth-soul and modify some of it into Soul-reproductive and the presence of Soul-reproductive makes the entity a living substance and we realize that life is Growth plus Reproduction. However Soul-corporeal and Soul-reproductive are found only in creation, whereas there is a huge excess of free and pure Growth-soul to be characterized as the all-becoming or Creative power.

In a Reincarnation Body the soul, and body as the vehicle of the soul, remain a loose mixture, since the soul may be entirely different in nature to that of the body. This may mean that the soul is not powerful enough to produce impacts upon its vehicle, the body, or make it more sublime in any way. The reverse is the case with the soul in a Resurrection Body. The soul is so powerful that the body, as its carrier, becomes sublime or soul-like, due to the impacts of soul upon matter. Now the body becomes soul-like. When thus transformed or refined, body becomes the fit vehicle of soul, which is another way of saying that matter has become soul-like and, as such, a mirror image of soul, when the two easily fuse into an indissoluble whole. Such a body and its soul make it Soul-incorporate which is a synonym of Resurrection Body; to look at it is a body but by virtues a soul, something like a nascent or active form of a gas otherwise inert.

In the above explanation we find Dualism and Monism as inevitable stages of each other. We can start with one Growth-soul and finally realize our body as the resultant of two donors but represents an indissoluble unity. Likewise Resurrection Body is Soul-incorporate, inseparable and as one. Pantheism on the contrary can account only for a Reincarnation Body.

Even the Chinese, who have developed Dualism most, in their cosmology start with Ch'i or Chhi as the one primordial entity, all-changing and all-becoming. Ch'i as entity is soul or at least self-expanding as vapour. The alchemist starts with Prime Matter which emphasizes its corporeal nature. When Oswald makes Energy = Matter, following him we can equate Ch'i = Prime Matter = Growth-soul, being our term for it. Once there is power of growth that of reproduction is implied, much as creation signifies both creation of matter and creation of life.

56. Positive conception of sub-souls.

A conception remains vague when it is purely hypothetical. The case becomes different when it appears as abstraction or deduction from some observable reality; this makes it a positive concept. To begin with soul is a positive idea for it is made to explain life and this in turn differentiates the living and the dead. The idea of a mono-elemental soul is unable to separate inorganic forms of matter from those that are living. Common to both is power of growth of some kind for even a crystal of alum can grow. Thus we arrive at the idea of a sub-soul as Growth-soul. This as the content needs a container or vehicle which becomes Soul-corporeal, an idea deduced from matter. Form and function, matter and energy, Growth-soul and Soul-corporeal become the inevitable minimum concepts if we are to conceive creation properly or formulate a system of cosmology. The dual elements are Spirit and Soul, or Brahman and Atman in Sanskrit. Had we started with this pair as such it would have been difficult to assign priority to Brahman or to Spirit but we have seen how easily we can start with Growth-soul and explain the birth of matter which otherwise conceived becomes Soul-corporeal. Given Growth-soul and Soul-reproductive, which characterize life, cosmogony starts with the assumption of Growth-soul, which as one, not related to any other, remains unknowable, but conceivable from what follows as Soul-corporeal. The birth of matter following energy, as the second, becomes knowable, and this in turn makes the idea of Growth-soul a positive one rather than merely hypothetical. With those two sub-souls we can explain creation but not yet life. When Growth-soul is partly modified by Soul-corporeal there also results Soul-reproductive which is necessary to explain how life began. Once there is creation life becomes a form of existence, and correspondingly Soul-reproductive a modification of Growth-soul. Hence we arrive at the idea that cosmogony is dependent upon two elements, Growth-soul and Soul-corporeal, and the former corresponds to Brahman and the latter to Atman in Sanskrit.

We are now required to show that the word Brahman, independently considered, should connote the idea of growth if we are to equate Growth-soul = Brahman. Bhide (96) has the root "Brah" = to grow, and "man" can be taken here for convenience as a suffix. The resultant word, Brahman, would then connote an entity that grows, implying, to grow = to be alive. Brahman, further conceived as soul, would be the life-conferring principle making Growth = Life. We must now look for support from a writer on alchemy. Sampson (39; 490) writes that, "the Archaeus, a personification of life force in all created things (organic or inorganic) was invented by Paracelsus and discussed by van Helmont to elucidate the putative volitional power of *matter to grow*, to resist disease, to heal and to reproduce itself". Archaeus then would be identical with Ch'i of the Chinese, and with Prime Matter of the alchemists in general. Moreover Sampson quotes Faber, as alchemist, maintaining that, "what others call Archaeus is nothing else than *seminal power* of every seed". And we have shown how Growth-soul is partly transformed into Soul-reproductive, the two genetically being the same. Thus if we have taken as complex Growth-soul-cum-Soul-reproductive, Faber attributes to Archaeus, *power to grow*, and also as having *seminal power.*

Needham (47; 226) equates the English and Chinese words, Life = Seng. We further learn from him that the original inscribed character of "Seng" is a "drawing of a plant rising out of the ground; symbolic of vegetal growth". People admit that what is seen is more impressive than what is heard. However the Sanskrit-Chinese pair of words, Brahman-Seng would constitute an audio-visual complex, confirming Growth = Life, Brahman as Growth, and Seng as life. Thus we are justified in interpreting Brahman as Growth-soul.

Jung (97; 345) discusses the etymology of the English word "soul" and its substitutes in other languages. They all signify air, but make air itself as something moving. Now Bhide (96) translates the word Air = Ats, which has as its root At = to move. This qualifies "the moving one" as Air. But the same suffix "man" as in Brahman appears again in Atman which signifies Breath, "the air moving in the body", when to breathe = to be alive, or possess a living body.

Thus Growth-soul or Brahman is of a general nature whereas Soul-corporeal or Atman clearly specific. We also realize that Growth is a far wider phenomenon than Breathing. On account of its more specific nature, suggesting a living body, we have deduced the idea of Soul-corporeal, but extended it as the reciprocal of Growth-soul since the soul was to be constituted of two sub-souls.

It is necessary however to support our deduced notion of Atman by what has been accepted in ancient times. Monier-Williams (31; 135) informs that, in Atharva-Veda, Atman signifies "the individual soul, self, abstract individual". Moreover in Sanskrit literature we often find Atman used in the sense, Atman = Body. On such a basis we are justified in our conception of Soul-corporeal as the sub-soul supplementing Growth-soul, with these two constituting soul as a whole. Having got to these two concepts we find Soul-corporeal as donor of form and of individual characters, whereas Growth-soul having the function of conferring life. We can therefore equate afresh, Brahman = Growth-soul and Atman = Soul-corporeal, which between themselves are further interrelated as function and form, and as content and container.

57. *Symbolism revealing alchemy as imitating creation.*

A wise judgment is based upon evidence offered by selected but all-informative witnesses. We likewise seek the minimum, if not even a single symbol, which is all-revealing as alchemy imitating creation. It is to be the one symbol of which every detail mutually supports the others and when integrated properly constitute the whole as creation. In an earlier article I (98) have reproduced three symbols with eggs, each to be considered as Cosmic Egg. The first is the design of Maier, dated 1617, taken from De Jong (89) showing an egg vertically placed which is obviously intentional for in this position it can be conceived as being cut longitudinally giving rise to two halves as mirror images. The Cosmic Egg carrying the Cosmic Soul would incorporate Yang and Yin or Brahman and Atman. Besides the egg stands a man with a lifted sword obviously representing the creator who, by *cutting* the egg, would "declare open" creation. Creation begins when there are two entities. The Pythagoreans grant that "one" is no number, for what is "one", though conceivable, is not knowable. That is also why we cannot know the original source of existence as one though we can positively conceive of its reality. The Pythagoreans therefore consider "two" as the first number. With two then begins creation.

The next symbol comes from a Latin work of 13th Cent. and is taken from Jung (92; fig. 98). According to him it shows "the philosophic egg whence the double (headed) eagle is hatched". It is best interpreted as the Cosmic Egg hatching to deliver an androgynous creator. There are two heads of the eagle bearing the crowns of king and queen. Bird is a symbol of soul and eagle, as solar-bird, easily represents the Cosmic Soul. Its two heads therefore represent the joint-elements of the Cosmic Soul, Brahman and Atman or Yang and Yin, opposites, but joint-creators. The egg from which such an androgynous creator is emerging can therefore only be the Cosmic Egg.

The third symbol is the ideal representation of Cosmic Egg found anywhere in the literature. I can only express my regret that it has never been taken seriously nor fully interpreted so far. It is the design of the alchemist, Jamsthaler, who offered it in 1625, and is taken from Jung (92; Fig. 199) and is offered here as fig. 7. Jung merely calls it "hermaphrodite on the winged globe of Chaos", which hardly does any justice to it. In the index Jung gives a few figures pertaining to eggs but fig. 199 is not among them. That the symbol primarily represents an egg and looks oval has been ignored. Nevertheless it is a clear representation of Cosmic Egg, containing all existence, the creator and his creation. Here I am reminded of the answer an intelligent school boy in America gave on being asked to explain the vacuum tube as reported by Shahin (99). The ingenious reply maintains that "a vacuum tube contains nothing. All of its parts are outside of itself". In fig. 7 we have the inverse picture, "there is nothing outside, all that exists, the creator and creation, are inside the egg". The first item to be looked for is the symbolism of Nothing. The Creator's Egg came out of Nothing, and Nothing is depicted as the dark background which ideally represents "Nothing". From Nothing emerged the Creator's Egg, which is obvious by its oval shape. The most important content of Cosmic Egg is the Creator. We have discussed the creator best as androgynous Shiva. In Jamsthaler's symbol, fig. 7, there is the androgynous Creator, as the hermaphrodite, labelled Rebis. Now the creator carries as his paraphernalia, a pair of magic wands of creation, the Compass held by the male half, and the Mason's Square held by the female half. Compass/Mason's Square have also become the emblem of Freemasonry and its history must likewise be traced to a cult of immortality with worship of the power of creation. However the Compass/Mason's Square symbolism is clearly of Chinese origin as I (91) have explained before. The hermaphrodite being human is the creator of microcosm. As the creator of macrocosm he has incarnated himself as the pair Sun/Moon, though separate, they are like the two poles of a magnet functionally two-as-one. As macrocosm creation is represented by the several planets shown. Then the hermaphrodite-creator has produced the four Cosmic elements from which the entire super-structure of the universe has taken shape. As the fifth element himself would be Creative Power. The four elements are like bricks that constitute every structure, organic or inorganic. Thus the contents of the Cosmic Egg show these four constituents as "embryonic elements" like seeds incorporating potentialities, and not representing the final realities. *Earth* is seen as globe, *Air* is represented as wings, *Water* as dragon, and *Fire* as flames emitted by the dragon from its mouth. Supplementing the Cosmic elements. Macrocosm is represented as creation represented by five planets, forming an arc with Sun-Moon. In the centre of this arc is placed the planet Mercury, just above the head of the androgynous Creator. By assigning such a position to the planet Mercury, really the homophonous metal, mercury, is meant, which is all-important in alchemy. Lastly there is minor pair of symbolism, and we must not overlook any detail. The globe is super-indicated by a geometrical pair of figures, a triangle pointing upwards and a square. Such a triangle represents the male principle. and the square the female. Thus triangle-square constitute a male-female "geometrical" hermaphrodite. Then the triangle is marked with number 3, and square with 4. Now odd numbers represent male and even female, so that "three-four" as "odd-even" symbolize an "arithmetical" hermaphrodite. Lastly there is a cross of four lines emanating from a circle with a dot. A circle, with or without a dot, symbolizes the sun, and this is the source of creative power, the sole creator in any system of paganism. Thus there are five points for five elements. The centre is occupied by a small circle within which there is again a miniature cross. The centre as the fifth element represents Creative Power and this is represented by the cross though indistinct due to its small size. The cross represents sun-moon the creator being a dual-natured entity. Budge (100; 338) deals with the significance of cross as a symbol of "heaven or some power of it", which can only be creative power, and among the various other forms he illustrates a cross like the one in the globe here, in fig. 7. Thus fig. 7 is saturated with symbolism of creative power and creation as the best symbol existing of the Cosmic Egg. We must not forget that the hermaphrodite or Rebis personifies the fifth-element, the Creative Power.

The symbol of Cosmic Egg easily fits in a classic on alchemy thereby confirming it as imitating creation. The legend of homunculus discussed by Eis (95) fully brings out this feature not otherwise obvious in an art supposed to make some particular alloy as gold. That such was "the chemical dream during the Renaissance" has also been clearly observed by Prof. Debus (101), He writes that "Paracelsus and his group were convinced that chemistry (alchemy) offered the true key to Nature that would unlock the secrets of heaven and earth". And when it unlocked the secrets of Heaven and Earth it unlocked the secrets of creative power. This is confirmed by Doré (102; vol. V, p. 512) pointing out that, "according to the Book of Changes, Yin-King, when Heaven and Earth exert their influences all things are transformed and vivified", for which the proper term would be exercising "creative power". Hence we can easily confirm that Heaven + Earth = Creator. In fact Doré (102; vol. V, p. ii) does observe that in China, "at present Heaven and Earth are worshipped instead of the creator". Debus finally concludes that the alchemist's "was a search for our Creator through his created work by chemical investigations". It is equally true to say that the search was directed to reveal powers of the creator which enabled the adept to imitate creation.

58. Concordance between Indian medicine and Indian philosophy.

Indian medicine is unique in recognizing at first rejuvenation, not only as possible, but assigning it priority over treatment of other ailments. Indian philosophy is unique in specializing as its aim to acquire immortality. Thus there is little difference in their objectives as rejuvenation-cum-immortality in this world and the same in post-mortem life. Medicine started as impact of Animism upon herbalism, when a plant became the donor of a quantum of mono-elemental soul adding the same to increase life-span. Medicine further developed on impact of Dualism upon herbalism, when a sub-soul of plant joined with the opposite sub-soul of metal and produced a herbo-metallic complex containing an ever-increasing soul of dual origin. But the soul as constituted in man was a loose mixture of its sub-souls. On the contrary the body was a perfect union of the two opposites to which it owed its origin, and thereby represented an element in its own right. Should the soul be reconditioned to compare itself in its make-up with the body, the former entering the body would become Soul-incorporate. However as facts are, body is an element whereas Spirit and Soul are a loose mixture of sub-souls. Briefly, Life = Body+Spirit+Soul. The alchemist tried to explain the existence of inorganic substances on the same basis. Al-Razi was the first to formulate that, Existence = Salt (Body)+Sulphur (Spirit)+Mercury (Soul). Salt was what resisted fire; it was like the ashes of a dead body. Sulphur was the most volatile principle and also the combustible. Mercury was less volatile and non-combustible. In Europe this theory was popularized by Paracelsus who is credited as its real author. However when sulphur and mercury form a loose mixture at best cinnabar results. This represents the soul of inorganic forms particularly of metals, all liable to rust and decay. Should sulphur and mercury combine as ideal opposites the resultant would be ever-lasting and ever-increasing as Ferment-gold, or its precursor, the right compound of activated sulphur and mercury, as Elixir, or Satva. But as art all attention was paid to making the Soul-corporeal sublime, the metal of herbo-metallic complex was calcined and pulverized and mercury of mercuro-sulphur complex was made fire-proof.

We now turn to Indian philosophy. European philosophy covers a large spectrum of knowledge. On the contrary Indian philosophy is specialized as the philosophy of immortality. As such historians of philosophy hesitate to consider Indian philosophy as philosophy at all. It is entirely dependent upon an ever-increasing soul which thus attaches utmost importance to its sub-souls and to their union as opposites. In Sanskrit, Spirit = Brahman and the Soul = Atman. Here Prof. Hiriyanna (103; 54) expressly writes that, "the two terms Brahman and Atman have been described as the two pillars (or opposites) on which rests the whole edifice of Indian philosophy", aiming at immortality. Whereas sulphur and mercury are the pillars on which rests alchemy, Brahman and Atman are the corresponding pillars on which rests Indian philosophy.

Thus there is perfect concordance between Indian medicine and Indian philosophy each unique because of specialized common aim as immortality. We shall be confirming the dependence of these systems upon two elements, or upon applied Dualism, by further considering Chinese religion and alchemy. We know otherwise that there were ascetics in China and they founded alchemy precisely with the same objective of rejuvenation-cum-immortality. Doré (104; vol. IX, p.2) refers to what the Chinese believe to be the first born. "He it is who teaches the doctrine that confers immortality. All who arrive at this knowledge must mount step by step to ever-lasting life, refine themselves like spirits and in the full light of day turn into immortals". We see firstly that the Chinese believed in acquiring immortality and that by sublimating or refining themselves or transforming corporeal entities into spiritual ones. And in order to become soul-like the previous "mortal soul" had to be reconditioned as leading to immortality. And this in effect depends upon union of opposites that are akin or supplementary to each other and not as any two entities. Here we learn from de Groot (105) that, "the union (note the word) Kwei (Atman) with Shen (Brahman) is the highest among all tenets (as also) the whole fundamental theory about the human soul in a nutshell". One can easily feel that the emphasis on Kwei and Shen is nothing less than on Brahman and Atman as found in Indian philosophy. And de Groot in the first instance also speaks of their union.

59. Union of opposites as a practical doctrine.

The theory has been explained that a mixture exists when two components are not equal. On the contrary when they are like mirror images there results union of opposites when Opposites = Co-creators and Union = Creation. Such a creation is ever-increasing and eternal. The theory with its applied form is shared by Indian philosophy and Indian medicine as also by Chinese philosophy and alchemy. The product of alchemy is Elixir, union between sulphur and mercury, or better still Ferment-gold, which is Elixir in the vehicle of gold. In any philosophy of immortality the counterpart of Elixir is Resurrection Body and not Reincarnation Body.

In this paragraph we wish to emphasize the practical phase of the theory of opposites as co-creators. In each case the material element, the counterpart of Soul-corporeal, has to be spiritualized or made sublime or soul-like, to function as the joint-creator or supplement, if not even as the mirror image of Growth-soul. Doré has offered a Chinese source where the spiritualization of matter is indicated. The practical systems of such spiritualization based on Indian philosophy have resulted in Yogic and Tantric exercises on which enough literature exists. Even Islam has developed a corresponding system called Sufism devoted to the acquisition of super-natural powers as prelude to immortality. John A. Subhan (106; 76) deals with Nafs, the Arabic word for Atman or Soul-corporeal, as distinct from Ruh or Brahman. Thereby he writes that, "there are among Sufis many outward methods of mortification such as fasting, silence and solitude". In as much as both alchemy and Sufism progressed on parallel lines, both aiming at immortality and both originated from China, we also find Chinese stressing on spiritualizing the corporeal man. Doré (102; vol. IX, p. 28) writes as follows: "To attain transcendent qualities (the conditions characterizing an aspirant of immortality) the first requirement is abstinence including the pleasures of the palate. Then the vital spirit, the essence of the constituent elements, Yin and Yang, must be strengthened in all ways possible with special diet, gymnastic and medicine. When maximum vital force has been secured methods must be devised for securing these and the adept has to *spiritualize himself to render himself independent of matter*". Nothing can be stated more clearly. Thus in all schools of mysticism Soul-corporeal is the sub-soul to which all attention is devoted and in doing so the aim is to make it as sublime as possible. For this mortification was deemed necessary which is shared by the Muslim Sufi and the Hindu Yogi alike. When Subhan further recalls a Sufi-saying implying such mortification is "death to self", it indirectly confirms, Self=Nafs=Soul-corporeal, which we have suggested before. Moreover the concept of "death to self" in Sufism has its counterpart in alchemy, where the corresponding term is "Kushta", killed, which means a despirited body, with the corpse intact, and far from having been annihilated. The metal as "Kushta" dies as something imperfect and liable to rust, but is resurrected as gold which is fire-proof. "Death to Self" does not connote the total destruction of any entity but of the "mortal" for it to be resurrected as "immortal" when the body becomes a Resurrection Body, or Soul-incorporate with matter now endowed with virtues of soul.

60. *Jabir's magic square and the importance of its four numbers*

A chapter may be added based on the article of Stapleton (1953) "On the numbers on which Jabirian alchemy was based". He refers to the two volumes on Jabir ibu Hayyan, the master of Islamic alchemy by Paul Kraus. Stapleton writes that "Kraus was able to prove that Jabirian alchemy was essentially an extension of the Pythagorean theory that *number is the basic* factor not only in the universe but of all that the universe contains...matter. Matter was made of all the four elements, Heat. Cold. Moisture and Dryness, arranged in varying proportions of the numbers. 1, 3, 5 and 8 but in the invariable total of 17."

Finally Stapleton observes that "Kraus in the end was unable to offer any definite reason why the four numbers in question were regarded by Jabir as being of such fundamental importance in the constitution of matter". Jabir offers a design as the magic square of three with these four numbers forming the left corner at the base. This figure is offered here as fig. 1, with additional markings to make the design more informative. Moreover Kraus also observed that the design Jabir's selected, he found "in more than one Jabirian treatise mentioned as facilitating child birth". Thus there are two main problems. Firstly the significance of the four numbers in the design, the magic square of three, and what has a charm that facilitates child birth to do with alchemy. What is the active principle in that design.

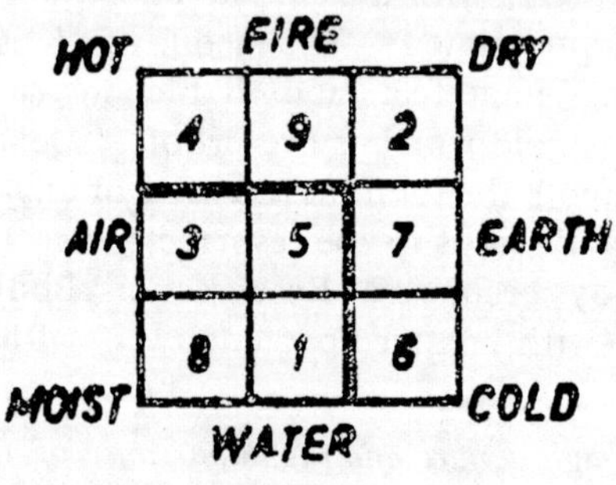

Fig. 1

In the first instance all depends upon number. Numerology arose in Babylon and a number was looked up as potential power. Pythagoras borrowed Babylonian numerology so that to solve any problem in this field we have to consider Babylonian sources. Now Venus was the brightest star and was considered as representing the Babylonian goddess of fertility. It was depicted as a five-cornered star with the corners duly numbered. As 1 to 5 amount to 15, this became the arithmetical designation of Venus. Thus Venus geometrically was symbolized as the magic square of 3 and arithmetically as 15. Then the numbers assigned to the magic square of three, counted as any series amounted to 15 as can be confirmed on examining fig. 1.

Moreover it would be observed that fig. 1 can also serve as the symbol of cosmology. This would be due to the Babylonian idea that "number is the basic factor in the universe" and cosmology deals with it. We have now to explain that four of its numbers impart importance to the whole design, fig. 1. In Chinese there is the term Sau-Pao, meaning three primordial powers. They are Heaven and Earth as joint producers and water is the first substance that was created. Water being the first to appear it has been assigned No. 1 in fig. 1. This settles the importance of one of the four important numbers mentioned above. Air came next and was given No. 3, the highest odd number after 1, cosmic elements are given odd numbers in fig. 1. To say that numbers 1 and 3 are important is to affirm that Water and Air are the most important cosmic elements. No less an authority than Von Helmont (1572-1627 A.D.) as Holmyond (1957; 192) informs has stated that "instead of the four elements of Aristotle there are two primitive elements, Water and Air. Of these two water is more active because from it all other substances except air are produced." When the importance of Water and Air is confirmed, the significance of Jabir's numbers 1 and 3 is revealed.

Now these two elements, Water ad Air share a quality in common and it is moisture, which is given No. 8 in fig. 1. As a result No. 8 of Jabir's four numbers is also shown to be important. We are now left with No. 5 of the four Jabirian numbers. It represents the source of creation. It is recognised that auspicious energy is produced by a pair of opposites. Thus 9 + 1 = 10 and 3 + 7 = 10. Here 5 is its own opposite like two twins appearing identical. It means 5 is its own opposite for 5 + 5 = 10 like any pair of opposites. This theory has been explained in 1970. The position of 5 in the centre explains its role in cosmogony. The Greeks would interpret the source of creation as ether which like the Chhi of Chinese is subtle matter changed with creative energy. With the above explanation the importance of No. 5 is also obvious. With it all these 4 numbers, 1, 3, 5 and 8 have been shown to be fundamental in cosmogony and thus in the make up of any form of matter.

We have mentioned that auspicious energy results in union of opposites. Then creative energy must result from the highest pair of opposites which means Heaven and Earth. They are symbolized in fig. 1 which contains then in their potential form: Earth is supposed to be square shaped. Even Rigveda 10.19.8 states that "four are the corners of the earth". Here fig. 3 shows its four corners, further possessing only even numbers, and symbolizes Earth. To find a symbol of Heaven we have to realize that its content is the cosmic soul and soul is symbolized as

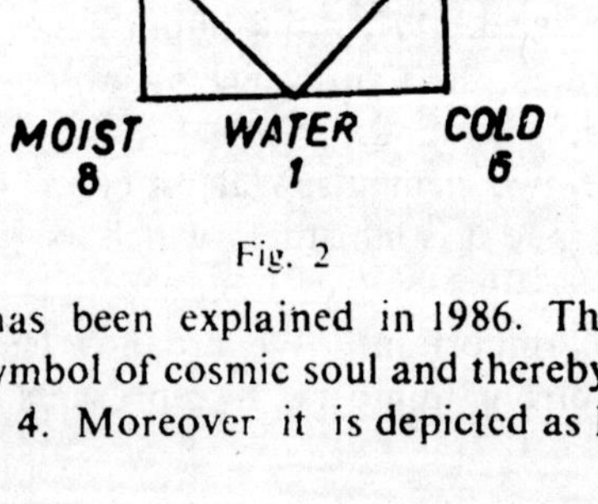

Fig. 2

cross which has been explained in 1986. Then the cross becomes the symbol of cosmic soul and thereby of Heaven, shown in fig. 4. Moreover it is depicted as having been

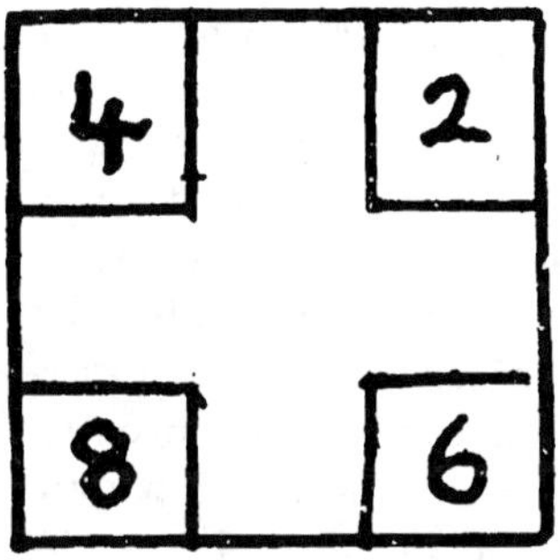

Fig. 3

Fig. 4

formed by only odd numbers while earth was formed by four even numbers. It will be noticed that fig. 3 contains a special cross which appears as fig. 4 decorated with odd numbers. Briefly stated figs. 3 and 4 are potentially included in fig. 1. Fig. 1 itself has resulted in union of the opposite squares as is shown in fig. 2. Here No. 5 is explained as representing ether, the primordial substance, as the source form of creation. When fig. 1 potentially incorporates figs. 3 and 4, the symbols of Earth and Heaven, it can produce auspicious energy which can be exploited to facilitate child birth or to facilitate changing a base metal into a noble one.

SUMMARY

In ancient times the aged was felt as a social parasite and exiled as an ascetic. His solitary life in a forest needed robust health which created dreams of rejuvenation. He gathered medicinal plants primarily to regain youth and next to cure other ailments. This unique feature is recognized by Charaka who about 200 A. D. first codified Indian medicine. The art of rejuvenation as also its drugs were called Rasayana. Moreover what rejuvenated also immortalized. Another ascetic, fearing death more than infirmity, wanted to be sure of immortality, be it in post-mortem life. He developed spiritual exercises which imparted super-human powers and thereby promised him immortality. Such an art has been called Rasayana by Patanjali. Thus Rasayana is the art of immortality, be it by medicaments or by spiritual exercises. The philosophy supporting spiritual Rasayana was Upanishads culminating in Vedanta. Accordingly, Indian medicine is unique in recognizing rejuvenation and Indian philosophy unique in aiming at immortality. These features pinpoint their common founder as the ascetic who has therefore left his stamp upon both the systems.

On account of his positive contributions we must endorse Bharata Iyer (107; 15) who maintains that "the Yogi (ascetic) is undoubtedly the most challenging and arresting figure in the cultural story of India".

When a single drug or Simple was used, according to Animism, the active principle was a quantum of soul which was transferred to the consumer to add to his strength. It was however a fixed quantum, bound to be exhausted. Animism made the soul mono-elemental which explained existence but not creation or generation. Later when man took to pastoral life he observed reproduction among animals leading to multiplicity and conceived of Dualism. Generalizing even soul became dual-natured. The male-soul, was Growth-soul and the female-soul, Soul-corporeal, the former responsible for life-span, the latter for form. The sub-souls are Spirit and the Soul in English, Brahman and Atman in Sanskrit. When disproportionate they remain as a loose mixture and man becomes mortal. But if well-balanced there results union of opposites into a hermaphrodite, an autonomous system, self-generating like a ferment. The possessor of such a soul becomes ever-lasting and if man, immortal. Such a theory is most conspicuous in a unique system where a male and female partake in sexual gymnastics, not for pleasure, but to generate a power which can be assimilated to increase longevity. Turning to medicine, a metal, as carrier of female sub-soul, was calcined with a plant, rich in male sub-soul, and the resulting calcined metal was a herbo-metallic complex, as the donor of an ever-increasing soul and thereby a drug of immortality. Killing a metal by heat and resurrecting it by a herbal-soul gives, not a calcined metal, but a Resurrection Body or Soul-incorporate. This makes man super-human and immortal.

According to an old idea Blood was soul and cinnabar, red as blood, was conceived as soul. Its two constituents Sulphur and Mercury became sub-souls. Their loose mixture made cinnabar but if properly combined, as mirror images, the resultant would be inseparable and ever-lasting as gold. Synthetic gold would be Ferment-gold and no Fossil-gold. It would be the ideal drug of immortality and became the target of alchemy. Even vermilion, or synthetic cinnabar, pulverized and levigated can become soul-like, which serves as panacea and a drug of rejuvenation. Such a product is Makara Dhwaja, the "Hallmark of Cupid" and sold in India today.

Then among drugs there were Simples, with large quanta of soul but as fixed amounts. Next calcined metals, including calcined gold, as herbo-metallic complexes, like a hermaphrodite by constitution and ferment by function, with soul ever-increasing and making man immortal. Finally mercury and sulphur, as sub-souls of metals, could be combined to produce an all-changing substance, an elixir, which can make things ever-lasting. When tested with base metals these can become gold and then Ferment-gold, itself as effective as elixir. Once man could admit a base metal becoming ever-lasting as gold, synthetic gold would become the ideal drug of immortality.

Even Indian philosophy depends upon Dualism where Brahman and Atman are sub-souls which must enter into union as opposites. Yogic exercises, apart from the sexual gymnastics indicated above, confer super-human powers, revealing that the soul had become ever-increasing and thereby all-changing. Man now acquires a Resurrection Body with its virtues which best assure him of a post-mortem immortality. When we compare Indian medicine with its Rasayana drugs, and Indian philosophy, with its importance attached to Brahman and Atman, we have parallel developments. Alchemy places all importance on sulphur and mercury the sub-souls of cinnabar, and it was born in China. Correspondingly Chinese religion considers Kwei (Atman) and Shen (Brahman) as sub-souls and their union as the most vital concept, and this again because there has been asceticism also in China.

BIBLIOGRAPHY

1. Taylor, F. Sherwood (1951).
The Alchemist.
2. Holmyard, E.J. (1957).
Alchemy, Penguin Books.
3. Hooykaas, R. (1957).
Review of Holmyard's Book, item 2 above.
Arch. Inst. Hist. Sci.; 39 : 151.
4. Wilson, W.J. (1951).
Review of Taylor's book, item 1.
Btn. Hist. Med.; 25 : 397.
5. Hopkins, A.G. (1934).
Alchemy, a Child of Greek Philosophy.
Columbia Univ. Press.
6. De Ridder A., and W. Deonna (1927).
Art in Greece. p. 143. K. Paul, Trench and Trubner.
7. Virchow, R. (1849).
Quoted in *Isis*; 1961; 52 : 436.
8. Nasr, S.H. (1973).
Alberuni as Philosopher—*Proc. Alberuni Inter. Cong.*; Karachi, Nov. 1973.
9. Alberuni (in India from 1017-1030 A.D.).
E.C. Sachau : Alberuni's India. 1888, Vol. II.
10. Peggs, J. (1831).
India's Cries to British Humanity.
11. Ray, Priyadaranjan (1956).
History of Chemistry in Ancient and Medieval India, p. 36. Calcutta.
12. Dhabar, B.N. (Reprinted in 1955),
Essays on Iranian subjects. p 27. Bombay.
13. Roth, R. (1884).
Wo Waechst der Soma.
Z.D.M.G.; 38 : 134.

14. Griffith, R.T.H. (1897).
Atharva-Veda, Vol. I, p. 252.
Extract pub. *Christ. Lit. Soc. for India*, Madras.
15. Ballantyne, J.R. (1898).
Vedanta Sara, p. 6.
Published by *Christ. Lit. Soc. for India*, Madras.
16. Enfield, W. (1819).
History of Philosophy, Vol. I, p. 443.
London.
17. Lloyd, J. Uri (1921).
History of Vegetable Drugs, Vol. I, pp. 85-88.
18. Moser, C. (1917).
The Flower of Paradise.
National Geog. Mag.; Aug. 1917, p. 173.
19. Panse, F. and W. Klages (1964).
Klinisch-psychopathologische Beobachtungen bei chronischen Missbrauch von Ephedrin.
Arch. Psy. u. Neurologie; 206 : 69.
20. Kapadia, B.H. (1959).
A critical interpretation and investigation of the epithets of Soma.
Privately published. Vallabh, Vidyanagar, India.
21. Stein, Sir A. (1932).
On the Ephedra, the Hum Plant and Soma.
Btn. School. Or. Stu. London Institution; Vol. 6 : 501.
22. Qazilbash, N.N. (1948).
Some Observations on Indian Ephedra.
Q. J. Pharm. Pharmacol. 21 : 502.
23. Mahdihassan, S. (1963).
Identifying Soma as Ephedra.
Pakistan J. Forestry; Oct. 1963, p. 370, with 4 figs.
24. Charaka (2nd Cent. A.D.).
Charaka Samita.
Tr. by Gulabkunverba Ayurvedic
Society, Jamnagar, India, 1949,
In six volumes; Vol. V quoted here.

25. Wasson, Gordon (1970).
Soma : Divine Mushroom, New York,
Article on "the search per Soma" in *Pharm. J.*; 205, No. 5579, p. 378.
26. Nicholson, Irene (No date).
Mexican Mythology. P. Hamlyn, London.
27. Bailey, Sir Harold W. (1972).
J.R.A.S.; No. 2, pp. 99-110.
28. Smith, F.P. (1871).
Materia Medica and Natural History of China, p. 175. Shanghai.
29. Ray, Praphulla Chandra (1903).
A History of Hindu Chemistry, in 2 Vols.
30. Dhar, Nil Ratan (1952).
An article in the symposium on the History of Science, New Delhi. Cyclostyled Publication.
31. Monier-Williams, Sir M. (1899).
A Sanskrit English Dictionary.
32. Sufi, G.M.O. (1949).
Kashmir, in 2 Vols. Karachi. Vol. 2, p. 494.
33. Harmann, D. (1968).
His findings summarized in
Pharma International; Stuttgart. Issue 4, p. 46.
34. Dikshit, M. G. (1952).
Beads from Ahichchatra,
Ancient India; No. 8, p. 50 and p. 63.
35. Lal, B.B. (1955).
Excavations at Hastinapura,
Ancient India; No. 10/11, plate LVI.
36. Friend, J. Newton (1961).
Man and the Chemical Elements, p. 18. p. 278.
37. Mahdihassan, S. (1972).
Colloidal gold as an alchemical preparation.
Janus; 58 : 112.
38. Davis, T.L. (1936).
Dualistic Cosmogony of Huan-Nan-Tze and the background of Chinese and European alchemy.
Isis; 25.

39. Sampson, H. (1943).
Dr. Faber and his celebrated cordial.
Isis; 34.
40. Mahdihassan, S. (1961).
Der Chino-arabische Ursprung des'
Worts Chemikalie. *Pharm. Ind.*; 23 : 515.
41. Mahdihassan, S. (1961).
Elixir, its significance and origin.
J. Asiatic Soc. Pak.; Dacca. 6 : 39.
42. Schep, J.A. (1964).
The Nature of Resurrection Body.
Erdemans Pub. Co., U.S.A.
43. Mahdihassan, S. (1965).
The Nature of two souls in Alchemy.
J. Asiatic Soc. Pak.; Dacca. 10 : 67.
44. Malinowski, Bronislav (1929).
Sexual life in Melanesia, 2 Vols. New York.
Review in *Isis*. 1930; 13 : 395.
See also
Ashley-Montagu, M. F. (1937).
Coming into being among Australian aborigines.
London.
Review in *Isis*. 1938; 29 : 193.
45. Bhagavat Singhjee, His Highness (1937).
A Short History of Aryan Medical
Science. Gondal. p. 137. p. 139.
46. Mukand Singh, Thakur (1893).
Treatment of superstitions (In Urdu),
entitled Ilajul-Awham, Jagat Press,
Aligarh. p. 19.
47. Needham, J. (1956).
Science and Civilization in China. Vol. 2.
48. Birket-Smith, K. (1960).
Primitive Man and his Ways.
Tr. by R. Duffell. London.
49. Waley, A. (1932).
Notes on Chinese Alchemy. *Btn. School. Or. Stu. London.*; Vol. 6.

50. Stein, Sir M.A.
Kalhana's *Rajtarangini*, 2 Vols.
Motilal Banarsidas, Delhi.
51. Winternitz, M. (1925).
Some Problems of Indian Literature.
Calcutta Univ. Press.
52. Stappleton, H.G. (1927).
Chemistry in Iraq and Persia in the 10th Cent.
Asiatic Soc.; Calcutta. p. 402.
53. Filliozat, J. (1958).
Isis; 49 : 363.
54. Foote, J.A. (1919).
Medicine Fakes and Fakers of all ages.
National Geog. Mag.; Nov. 1919, p. 71.
55. Mookerji, Bhudeb (1927). Rasa-Jala-Nidhi,
Or Ocean of Indian Chemistry and Alchemy.
Calcutta. Vol. II, pp. 57, 118 and 293.
56. Temple, R.C. (1884-5).
Panjab Notes and Queries.
A.H. Tucker : Note 459, p. 52, Vol. I. (1884).
M. Millett: Note 460, p. 52 and Note 852, p. 111, Vol. I. (1884).
G. Woulfe : Note 1073, p. 204 Vol. II. (1885).
57. Claverley, E.E. (1936).
Encycl. Islam.; Vol. III, p. 828.
58. Nilsson, M. P. (1949).
A History of Greek Religion.
59. Taslimi, Manuchehr (1954).
An examination of Jildaki's
Nihayat Al Talib. Doctorate
Thesis. London Univ. Not Published.
60. Davis, T. L. (1943).
The Chinese beginning of Alchemy,
Endeavour; 2 : 154-160.
61. Mahdihassan, S. (1957).
Alchemy with Jinn, Sufi and Suffa as loan words from the Chinese.
Iqbal (Lahore); 7 : 1-10

62. Postans, Mrs. (1839).
Cutch. London. p. 197.
63. Aga, Hyder Hassan (1948).
Preface to Mrs. Wiqarunnisa Begum's Urdu book on Cookery, "Pakwan", Inthezami Press, Hyderabad, India.
64. Amartha-Chandrika (1906).
A Sanskrit-Bengali Dictionary, Calcutta. Page 242, Line 338.
65. Gossain, H.M. (1912).
Bengali to Bengali and English Dictionary. Calcutta.
pp. 820-821.
66. Mitra?
Bengali to Bengali Dictionary. Calcutta.
My copy has lost its title page. p. 26 and p. 454.
67. Gildemeister, J. (1876).
Alchymie,
Z.D.M.G.; 30 : 537.
68. Edkins, J. (1884).
Religion in China.
69. Mahdihassan, S. (1961).
Alchemy in the light of its names in Arabic, Sanskrit and Greek,
Janus; 49 : 79.
70. Read, J. (1937).
Prelude to Chemistry.
71. Gordon, D.H. (1939).
Buddhist Origin of Summerian Heads from Memphis.
Iraq; 6 : 37-38.
72. Abdul Hamid (no date).
Adhunik Bangla Rachana. Dacca. p. 24.
73. Bhushan, Mrs. Jamila Brij (1958).
Costumes and Textiles of India. Bombay.
74. Siecke, Ernst (1908).
Hermes der Mondgott.
Publishers: J.C. Hinrich. Leipzig.

75. Nilakanta Sastri, K.A. (1957).
Cultural Heritage of India, Vol. IV.
Rama Krishna Mission, Calcutta.
76. Agrawala, V. S. (1948).
Terracottas of Ahichchatra.
Ancient India; No. 4, p. 104.
77. Coomaraswamy Ananda (1916).
Rajput Painting.
Fig. 1 directly taken from Shanti Swarup's Arts and Crafts of India and Pakistan. 1957. p. 78.
78. Thompson, G. (1954).
Studies in Ancient Greek Society.
79. Watt, Sir G. (1903).
Industrial Exhibition at Delhi.
80. Sohoni, S.V. (1960).
Kartikeya Coin-type of Kumaragupta I.
Ind. Numis. Chronicle; 1 : 37.
81. Pagel, W. (1951).
Isis; 42 : 46.
82. Mallowan, M.E.L. (1947).
Excavations at Brak and
Chagar Bazar. *Iraq*; 9 : 120-21.
83. Miller, Harry (1970).
The Cobra.
National Geog. Mag. Sep. 1970.
84. Crawford, O.G.S. (1957).
The Eye goddess.
85. Das Gupta, Kalyan Kumar (1953).
Bisalki Temple at Bajwa, Hugly Dt.
J. Ind. Soc. Or. Arts: 19 : 43, 48.
86. Marshall, Sir John (1960).
The Buddhist Art of Gandhara. Fig. 17.
87. Read, J. (1957).
Through Alchemy to Chemistry.
p. 63, Fig. 19.
88. Splendor Solis (1582).
Edited by "J.K." Trubner and Co.,
London (No Date)

89. De Jong, H.M.E. (1969).
Michael Maier's, Atlanta Fugiens
First printed in 1617, p. 384, Fig. 8.
90. Rambach and De Golish (1955).
The Golden Age of Indian Art
5th-12th Cent. Taraporewala.
Bombay. Plate 26.
91. Mahdihassan, S. (1962).
Ueber einige Symbole der Alchemie.
Pharm. Indus.; Aulendorf. 24 : 41-45. Fig. 7.
92. Jung, C.G. (1953).
Psychology and Alchemy.
The edition of 1970, Fig. 199, does away with the dark background of the original.
93. Holzmann. A. (1884).
Brahman in Mahabharata
Z.D.M.G.; 38 : 198.
94. Brihadranayaka Upanishad (1951).
Sanskrit text and translation.
Ramakrishna Math, Madras.
95. Eis, G. (1967).
The Homunculus in Folklore and Legend.
Abbotempo. Book 4, p. 18.
96. Bhide, V.V. (1926).
A Concise Sanskrit-English Dictionary. Poona.
97. Jung, C. G. (1960).
Structure and Dynamics of the Psyche
Jung's Collected works. Vol. 8., p. 345.
98. Mahdihassan, S. (1972).
Imitation of creation by alchemy and its corresponding symbolism.
Abr Nahrain, Leiden, Vol. XII, pp. 99-117
see Figs. 1, 2 and 4.
99. Shahin, J. (1967).
Dow Europe: Growth is a Way of Life.
Diamond; 50(4) : 6
Pub. The Dow Chemical Co.,
U.S.A.

100. Budge, Sir E.A. Wallis (1961).
Amulets and Talismans. pp. 338-9.
101. Debus, A.G. (1968).
The Chemical Dream of the Renaissance,
Heffer, Cambridge, England. pp. 7 and 32.
102. Dorė, H. (1918).
Chinese Superstitions.
103. Hiriyanna, M. (1932).
Outlines of Indian Philosophy.
104. Doré, H. (1921).
Chinese Superstitions. Shanghai, Vol. IX, p. 2.
105. De Groot, M. J. J. (1892).
Religious System of China.
Vol. IV; pt. ii, p. 3.
106. Subhan, John A. (1938).
Sufism. Lucknow.
107. Bharata Iyer, K. (1958).
Indian Art, a short introduction,
Asia Publishing House. Bombay.
108. Dr. Baloch, Nabi Baksh Khan (1964).
Tarikh-i-Taheri: History of the town of Thatta,
by Syed Taher Thattvi. 1621.
Edited by Dr. Baloch. Published by Sindi
Adabi Board. Hyderabad Sind.
109. Sarton, G. (1942-3).
Isis; 34 : 176.
110. Holmyard, E.J. (1957) *Alchemy*.
111. Mahdihassan, S. (1970)
Union of Opposites, a Basic Theory in Alchemy and its Interpretation. Prof. Altheim Festschrift, Berlin pp. 251-263.
112. Mahdihassan, S. (1986)
Cross as the Symbol of Soul.
Pak. Archealogy No. 22:282-292.
113. Mahdihassan, S. (1988)
The Ideal Magic Square and its Evolution.
J. Central Asia 11(2): 59-70.

114. Mahdihassan, S. (1989)
Venus Arithmetically Designated as 15 *and Geometrically as the Magic Square of* 3.
J. Central Asia 12(2): 109-119.

115. Stapleton, H.E. (1953)
Probable Sources of the Numbers on which Jabirian Alchemy was Based. Arch. Intern. Hist. Sci. UNESCO, Paris. No. 22:44-59.

EXPLANATION OF FIGURES

Note: figures are given after this explanatory note.

FIG. 1: Shiva, charming as Cupid, with his spouse Parvati, was an infirm old ascetic before his marriage. He is Moon-god bearing Crescent as his insignia. And Moon-god is sovereign of herbs, growing on earth and the choicest on moon. The serpent around his body is the emblem of rejuvenation. From Coomaraswamy (77).

FIG. 2: Shiva filtering a herbal extract helped by Parvati. Snake, the emblem of rejuvenation, is conspicuous. The bull also represents fertility. A Raja of Kashmir is seen standing in full adoration. From a Kashmir enamel. From Watt (79).

FIG. 3: Shiva as master-herbalist and ascetic. A pot of herb in one hand is befitting a herbalist. Diagonally across his chest is a leaf inscribed on a ribbon as badge duplicating the pot of herb as emblem. In another hand is a lotus flower with lotus seeds forming a beaded circle. Lotus is unique as the only plant that produces young germinated plants and serves as the symbol of self-creation and reproductive power. It thus also characterizes Shiva. From Agrawala (76).

FIG. 4: Makara- half crocodile and half fish. Each symbolizes reproductive power to be equated as creative power. A semi-nude young woman bearing a child suggests that she is by no means sterile. She duplicates Makara as the symbol of fecundity. From Marshall (86).

FIG. 5: Cupids as alchemists preparing medicaments which would deserve to be stamped with "Cupid's Hallmark". The drugs would rejuvenate and make the consumer attractive to women or Cupid-like. From Read (87).

FIG. 6: Androgynous Shiva as creator. The alchemists also personify creative power as a hermaphrodite, with Reproduction = Creation, and the Creator = Hermaphrodite or an Androgynous deity. From a 6th Cent. Indian sculpture. From Rambach (90).

FIG. 7: Cosmic Egg emerging from Nothing. Nothing is symbolized as the dark background. The Egg is revealed by a clear oval outline. The creator is the androgynous Rebis. The magic wands of creation are the pair of Compass and Mason's Square, together the emblem of Freemasonry. The Compass symbolizes the principle of masculinity and the Mason's Square that of feminility, thus the two instruments represent an "androgynous" pair. The hermaphrodite, Rebis, being human, clear y represents the creator of microcosm. Incarnating himself as the pair, Sun-Moon, like the two poles of a magnet, the symbol represents the creator of macrocosm. The products of creation are the Cosmic Elements: Globe = Earth, Wings = Air, Dragon = Water, and Flames issuing from the Dragon's mouth = Fire. Rebis, himself represents the fifth element. Macrocosm as such is depicted by the five planets of which mercury, is on the top of the androgynous Rebis. This position is assigned to mercury for it is homophonous with mercury, the element of great significance in alchemy. On the globe the triangle and square form a "geometrical" pair of opposites when Opposites = Co-creators. Likewise the numbers, 3 and 4, constitute the "odd-even" pair as an "arithmetical" hermaphrodite. Lastly there is a horizontal and a vertical line as a cross when this symbolizes heaven implying its creative powers. Designed by Jamsthaler in 1625. From Jung (92).

FIG. 8: Bundle of grass placed horizontal. Both ends of grass have be dipped.

FIG. 9: An ephedra plant growing near Quetta. It contains rod shaped stalks, with no leaves.

FIG. 10: A bundle of seven ephedra plants, placed vertically in contrast to bundle of grass placed horizontally.

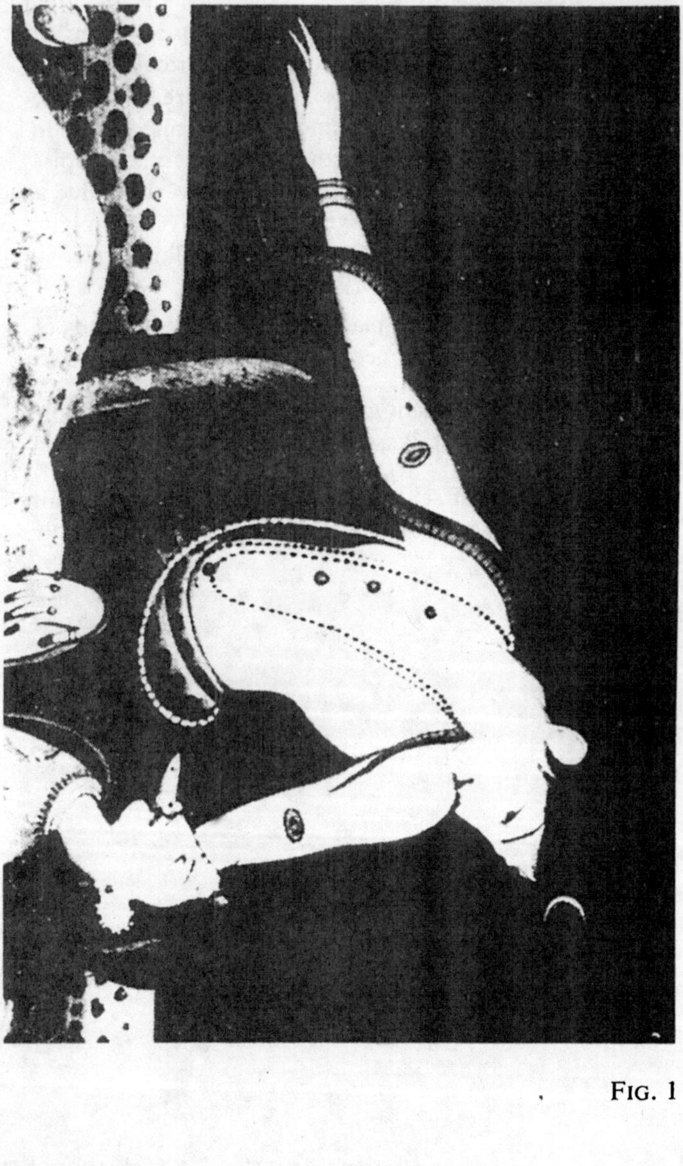

FIG. 1

FIG. 2

FIG. 3

FIG. 4

FIG. 5

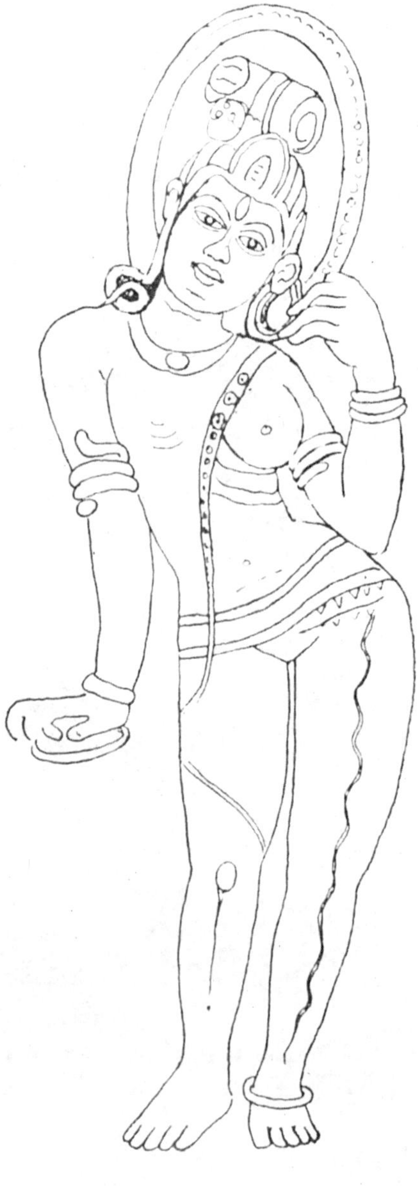

FIG. 6

FIG. 7

FIG. 8

FIG. 9

FIG. 10